T0329186

# A SON OF TWO COUNTRIES

## The Education of a Refugee from Nyarubuye

Casmir Mushongore Rubagumya

MKUKI NA NYOTA

DAR – ES – SALAAM

PUBLISHED BY
Mkuki na Nyota Publishers Ltd
P. O. Box 4246
Dar es Salaam, Tanzania
www.mkukinanyota.com
© Casmir Mushongore Rubagumya, 2017

ISBN: 978-9987-75-345-1

Visit www.mkukinanyota.com to read more about and to purchase any of
Mkuki na Nyota books.

You will also find featured authors, interviews and news about other publisher/
author events. Sign up for our e-newsletters for updates on new releases and other
announcements.

# Dedication

For all the children of Tanzania and Rwanda,
the hope of tomorrow

# Contents

# Acknowledgements

I am indebted to several people who, in one way or another, helped me in the process of writing this book. My family encouraged me to write my story for the sake of the current and subsequent generations of the Rubagumya family. My elder brother, Louis, played a big part, especially in jogging my memory on events that took place when I was very young. Prof. Josephat Rugemalira, Prof. Ludovick Kinabo and Henry Safari read earlier drafts of the manuscript and gave me very useful comments which helped me to improve it. In the process of publishing this book, the team at Mkuki na Nyota Publishers were very helpful and undertook the task efficiently and professionally. I especially thank the editors: Dr. Lisa María Noudéhou for extensive and very useful comments on the draft and Ms. Godance Andrew for handling all the logistics in the process of publication.

# Preface

Usually one expects authors of autobiographies to be rich and famous, people like politicians and movie stars. So why would a simple teacher like me want to write his autobiography? My motivation is to let my children and my grandchildren know their roots. I wish to have a written record of my life that those who come after me in the family tree are able to read and understand their origins. Later, after writing my personal story, I realised that it could speak to the youth of Tanzania and Rwanda as well.

There are three main points that I wish to make through this simple narrative. First, I want to encourage my children to write their own stories in order to have a written record that successive generations can read to understand where they came from. Whereas in Europe and North America some people have written records of their family history going back for centuries, in Africa we are still dependent on oral narratives. I think it is high time we also started keeping written records, since we no longer maintain oral tradition.

Second, I want to highlight the absurdity of national boundaries in Africa as demarcated by the Berlin conference. My life story shows these boundaries to be a detrimental farce. My father was from Rwanda, my mother from Burundi. Growing up in Karagwe, Tanzania, I had two aunts married to Tanzanians. For all these people, colonial boundaries meant nothing. In those days, there was free movement of people and intermarriages across boundaries. My surname, Rubagumya, bears testimony to the artificiality of these boundaries. It is found in Rwanda, north-western Tanzania and south-western Uganda. One day I was at Entebbe airport in Uganda and the immigration officer checking my passport said to me jokingly: "you have the wrong passport". I did not understand him at first. When I asked him why, he said Rubagumya was a Ugandan name. He was right and wrong: yes, Rubagumya is a Ugandan name, but it is also a Tanzanian and a Rwandese name; and no, I didn't have the wrong passport.

The same colonialists who divided up Africa in Berlin later re-drew the map of Africa in Versailles in 1919, again without consulting the Africans. After the 1st World War, what had been German East Africa (present day Tanzania mainland, Rwanda and Burundi) was partitioned into two territories. Tanganyika went to the British, while Ruanda-Urundi went to the Belgians. Had this new partition not taken place, I would be writing an entirely different story.

I only hope that current efforts by the people of East Africa to form the East African Federation will go a long way to making right these past historical inconveniences imposed on us by colonialists. The people of East Africa have more things in common than those that divide them. Unfortunately, our political leaders focus on the things that divide us, instead of those that unite us. That is why, in my view, progress towards the East African Federation is rather slow. However, this is another story.

The third point I want to make is that no matter how difficult circumstances may be, it is always possible to do something in life. The fact that I became a refugee at the age of 15 did not mean the end of my life. Through a combination of God's grace, good luck and hard work, I was able to advance academically until I became a university professor. The message I want to give to my children, my grandchildren, and the youth of Tanzania and Rwanda is that challenges in life should not discourage us; they should propel us to try and do our best to overcome. When you fall down, don't remain on the ground. Get up, dust off and start walking again, no matter how difficult the journey. I believe in God, but I don't believe in fatalistic attitudes towards life. Everything that happens to us is not the will of God. We cannot just sit down and wait for God to do everything for us. Julius Nyerere, the founding father of Tanzania, once said he refused to believe in a god who is ignorant, poor and ill. How can we believe that African children dying of malaria before the age of five is God's will? How can we believe that the scourge of HIV/AIDS on the African continent is God's will? If we believe this, we will be saying that God is racist; but the concepts of racism and God's goodness and perfection are mutually exclusive. If God created human beings in his own image, then ignorance, poverty and ill health cannot be God's will. These are problems that face our societies and us individually; individual and communal efforts can solve them. Being fatalistic is running away from our responsibilities as human beings.

My story, therefore, is the story of a refugee boy from Rwanda who grew up in Tanzania and later acquired Tanzanian citizenship. I narrate my trials and triumphs, both in Rwanda and Tanzania. In looking back, I try to understand who I am and the contribution of both countries to my identity as a human being.

Apart from my offspring, I hope my students will be able to read this story. These are from St. Peter's Seminary, Morogoro (1971-1972); Tabora Girls Secondary School (1973-1979); the University of Dar es Salaam (1982-2008); the University of Dodoma (2008-2013); and St. John's University of Tanzania (2013- ). It is said that teachers are king makers. I believe many of the students who passed through my hands have become 'Kings' and 'Queens'. I always become happy when I come across a former student of mine who has made it in life. I know I have helped to produce bishops, members of parliament, professors like me, famous lawyers, teachers and many more. I see this as a little contribution that I have made to humanity.

I also hope that some of my own teachers will be able to read this book. I would like to think that I am also a 'small king'; I am who I am today because of their efforts. I thank them immensely for shaping me intellectually and spiritually. My shortcomings in life are not because of their failings, but because of my weakness as a human being.

More generally, I hope people who read this story will understand what it means to be a refugee. Usually refugees are either despised or pitied. However, refugees are human beings like any other human beings. They certainly have challenges in life, but they also have their lives to live and they can achieve something in life. So far, many people have written about the survivors of the 1994 Rwanda genocide. To the best of my knowledge, no one has written about the experiences of Rwandese refugees in the diaspora. My story is a contribution in that direction.

I have tried to be as objective as possible in this story. However, the fact that I was a refugee for 18 years and was reminded of my origins long after I acquired Tanzanian citizenship will most probably be obvious in the tone of my story. Nonetheless, this is not a story of bitterness. It is a story of hope. Whatever happened to me and to the hundreds of thousands of other refugees from Rwanda is now history; but we need to learn from that history. The history of Rwanda is not a history of black and white. Certainly both Hutu and Tutsi have a responsibility for looking back, not in order to seek revenge, but to find out the truth of what happened and seek reconciliation. While it is necessary to punish those responsible for the 1994 genocide, it is equally necessary for both Hutu and Tutsi to do some soul searching and remove the seeds of mutual distrust and hatred from their hearts. It is especially important to ensure that those seeds of mutual suspicion and hatred are not planted in the young minds of future generations of Rwandese people. Unless this is done, I am afraid I can predict more cycles of violence, each new one more ferocious than the previous one. I am, however, also optimistic that, collectively, we will not let this happen. Let us take a leaf from the books of people like Nelson Mandela. His 27 years in prison with hard labour did not derail him from his conviction that South Africa belongs to every South African, regardless of their race. Likewise, every Rwandese should defend the principle that Rwanda belongs to all citizens of that country – Hutu, Tutsi and Twa.

When all is said and done, the challenges of Rwanda are not the challenges of ethnicity *per se*. They are the challenges of struggle for power over a span of several centuries. In 1896 the Rucuncu *coup d'état* in which King Mibambwe IV Rutarindwa was removed by the powerful Chief Kabare of the Abega clan and replaced by Kabare's nephew Yuhi Musinga (Yuhi V of Rwanda), was a result of the power struggle between two Tutsi groups. In 1973, Major-General Juvénal Habyarimana overthrew a fellow Hutu, President Grégoire Kayibanda. Habyarimana in turn consolidated his power and made sure it was concentrated in the hands of a few trusted relatives nicknamed akazu (a small house), thus alienating many of his fellow Hutu countrymen and women. Currently, President Paul Kagame's opposition does not only come from Hutu politicians; there are also Tutsi politicians, who at one time were very close to him, who are now part of the opposition to his rule. Although some historical events are narrated in this book, my intention is not to write the history of Rwanda or Tanzania. I have narrated these events, as accurately as I can, only as they touched my life in both countries. Those interested in the history surrounding these events will have to look elsewhere. Precisely because of this limitation, my story may feel disjointed because it jumps from one place to another. However, this is inevitable given the nature of the story itself.

For me the central symbol of this story is the Nyarubuye Roman Catholic Church. First, the Nyarubuye church evokes memories of my childhood as an altar boy and of my father as a clerk at the mission station. Secondly, the church has come to symbolize in Rwanda the worst atrocities of the 1994 genocide. For me, it is therefore an emblem of both childhood innocence and the subsequent dark spot in the history of my country of origin.

All the names in this book are real to the best of my knowledge and recollection, unless otherwise stated. If anything I say about any individual is interpreted negatively, I wish to apologize for that in advance, because this is not my intention.

# Note to the Reader

For those not very familiar with Rwanda, I need to say something about the meaning of Hutu and Tutsi, terms that appear quite frequently in this book. Who are the Hutu and who are the Tutsi? This question has been a subject of controversy among historians, so I cannot pretend that I will give a definitive answer here. There are two divergent schools of thought. One is that the Hutu and Tutsi are one and the same people, and that this distinction was created by Belgian colonialists in order to 'divide and rule' the people of Rwanda. The other school of thought is that the Hutu and Tutsi are two distinct ethnic, even racial, groups who migrated into present Rwanda from different directions and at different historical epochs. According to this latter school of thought, the Tutsi probably migrated from southern Ethiopia around the 13th century. By the 14th century, the original Tutsi-led monarchy in central Rwanda had been established (Rusagara 2009). They are supposed to be tall and slender, with oval faces and long, narrow noses. They came with their long-horned cattle and conquered the Hutu, who are short and stocky and were already settled agricultur – alists when the Tutsi came. These physical characteristics are, however, stereotypes which are rather elusive to pinpoint objectively. How tall is tall, and how does one determine a 'long narrow nose'? I know of very tall Hutus and very short Tutsis, so these descriptions are not very helpful.

The two schools of thought have critics. Saying the two groups are one and the same people is obviously not quite correct, since there are observable physical differences. However, these differences have been explained in terms of diet and natural selection. It is said that the average Tutsi is taller than the average Hutu because of a rich diet of milk enjoyed by the Tutsi over centuries. Saying that the two groups are distinct ethnic or racial entities is not true either. The two speak the same language, Kinyarwanda, have the same culture, and live together in the same communities. There is no Hutuland or Tutsiland in Rwanda. Even if it is assumed that they came from different origins, there have been intermarriages between the two groups for centuries. Also, in pre-colonial and colonial Rwanda, it was possible for one to move from one group to another, depending on one's socio-economic and/or political status. A Hutu could become a Tutsi through the process of *kwihutura* if he had access to cattle, got married to a Tutsi, or got an important political position. Likewise, if a Tutsi became poor, especially if he had no cattle, he would be regarded as Hutu. Mahmood Mamdani has suggested that the Hutu and Tutsi are a single cultural community, a community of Kinyarwanda speakers, but two different state-enforced political entities. In pre-colonial and colonial Rwanda, he argues, to be Tutsi was to be identified with power – both political and economic, while to be Hutu was synonymous with being a subject without economic and political power.

During the 1994 genocide, apart from looking at someone's physical features to determine whether they were Tutsi or Hutu, the perpetrators of genocide also used identity cards. During the colonial period and up to 1994, every Rwandese person was supposed to carry an identity card, which identified the bearer as Hutu, Tutsi or Twa. During the 100 days between April and July 1994, to carry a Tutsi identity card was to carry a death sentence in one's pocket.

# Chapter One

# Childhood

## Nyarubuye: The Peasant Life of a Prince

I went back to Nyarubuye in 1997 after 37 years of absence from my native land. I had just learnt that my father was dead. My homecoming was therefore not a happy one. I had not seen my father for several years, and I was not even able to bury him because, by the time I arrived, he had already been buried. In the village, since there are no facilities for treating a body, people are usually buried the same day they die. I could only visit his grave.

Nyarubuye was an unknown, nondescript little rocky hill in eastern Rwanda near the Rwanda-Tanzania border until 1994, when it became infamous for the genocide atrocities that took place inside its Catholic Church. It is estimated that about 20,000 people were massacred in and around the church in two days, the 14th and 15th April 1994. I was born on that hill – for in Rwanda, a country of a thousand hills, you talk about hills not villages – on 9th December 1946 and was baptized a few weeks after my birth, in the same church where the genocide atrocities were to be committed some 48 years later.

I was born in a devout catholic family. At that time, the majority of people in Rwanda were devout Catholics, at least in appearance. The Catholic Church in Rwanda had permeated the whole social fabric, so much so that the catholic greeting Yezu akuzwe/ iteka (Praise Jesus/ forever) had become a national greeting for everyone, including Muslims. In my case, not only was I baptized into the Catholic Church, my father, Aloys Rubagumya, happened to be a clerk at the Nyarubuye catholic mission. His family was therefore expected to be a role model Christian family. My mother, Generosa Bukuru, came from Burundi. One of my paternal aunts lived in Burundi, and she made arrangements for my mother to come to Nyarubuye, where she met my father and they got married.

My childhood was not very different from that of many other children on the hill. I say not **very** different deliberately, because families around our home perceived us as different. First, my father was a clerk at the catholic mission. He was getting a steady income, albeit a meagre one.

This could not be said of other families on the hill. Secondly, he had a few head of cattle, and therefore he was relatively better off than many other villagers around, who just depended on peasant agriculture for their livelihoods. It also needs to be said that owning cattle was not only important as a source of milk, it was, more importantly, an emblem of being a Tutsi and therefore "superior" to Hutu neighbours. Thirdly, we were living in a "European" house made of stone and roofed with tiles, one of the perks my father got for being a clerk at the catholic mission, while all our neighbours were living in nyakatsi – grass thatched huts. However, the house was no more than just two tiny bedrooms and an equally tiny living room. Needless to say, we had no running water and no electricity.

Our family traces its roots from a long line of nobles, descendants of Kimenyi, the last King of Gisaka in eastern Rwanda. So, for our neighbours we were not just Tutsi, we were also of a royal family! I can trace my ancestry to Kimenyi and beyond. I am Mushongore (my great, great grandfather's name that was given to me at birth), son of Rubagumya, son of Kadogo, son of Rwagaju, son of **Mushongore,** son of Mukotanyi, son of Kakira, son of **Kimenyi,** son of Bazimya, son of Ruregeya…of the Abagesera (also known as Abazirankende) clan. I was also given the praise name of Rusiribana, which was the praise name of Mushongore. The long form of Rusiribana is *"Rusiribana nabisize agahama rwa kirarama, izigisaza nazinyaze kigisambagana."*

Praise names were mainly used to identify a person's exploits during wars that took place at different historical epochs in Rwanda. This particular name praises Mushongore, who was so brave that he did not wait for his enemies to die before he took their cattle as booty.

By coincidence, my Christian name, Casmir, also happens to be the name of a Polish Prince. St. Casimir [or Kazimierz in Polish] (1458-1484) is the Patron Saint of Poland and Lithuania. The meaning of the name is given as "destroyer of opponents' glory during battle" or alternatively, "one who reveals and establishes peace" (Wikipedia). Why I was given this name, I don't know. Perhaps I am a victim of what Ngũgĩ wa Thiong'o, a renowned Kenyan writer, calls the dismembering project by Europe; trying to delete everything African from the African memory and replacing it with a European memory. Were we, Africans, given European names in order to be uprooted from our African culture? This could well be the case, but I don't think I am less African because I bear a European name. Nor was, for example, Mobutu Sese Seko Kuku Ngbendu wa Zabanga more African than Julius Nyerere because the former ditched his European name, Joseph-Desiré, while the latter didn't. Whatever its demerits, I was given a European name at baptism, and this is part of my identity. I don't consider myself less African because of this name.

A number of my family members are known for special skills. My grandfather, Kadogo, was well known for his medical skills. For example, we are told that one of his daughters was born prematurely. He made an incubator for her. This was a small trench dug near the fire place. Millet chaff was put in the trench, covered by soft inner leaves of a banana plant. The baby was put inside, with the same covering of soft banana leaves and millet chaff. She was fed inside the trench and monitored around the clock until full term. She was then removed from the incubator and grew up a normal baby. My aunt, despite this difficult beginning, was over 80 years old when she died.

Another heritage that I am proud to be associated with is artistic. At the beginning of the 19th century, Kakira, son of Kimenyi, from whom I am descended, invented the art of embellishing houses and thus making them more attractive. While traditional houses are on the decline in popularity, the Kakira Association in Gisaka has adapted the ancient art form into more modern products, the *imigongo* of Rwanda. Dominated by black, brown and white whorls and other geometric abstractions, the unique art works are now very famous in Rwanda, and many tourists buy them as souvenirs when they visit the country. My cousin Speciosa Gacurigwegwe is well known for her skilful hand in making *imigongo*.

At the time of writing, she is the Chairperson of the Kakira Association. Talking of royalty, I have other royal connections. One of my aunts, Nyiramakomari, married Mutara III Rudahigwa, the King of Rwanda from 1931 to 1959. She was later divorced, accused of being barren. However, she married another man and bore children by her second marriage! King Mutara III married another woman; they did not have any children. My other aunt, Gertrude Mushyankwano, married the last *Omukama* (Chief) of Karagwe, Bernard Itogo Ruhinda.

Despite all my royal connections, as a child I had many rural responsibilities. I helped my parents with all the village chores like fetching water from the village stream and collecting firewood from the eucalyptus plantation, which was a few hundred metres from my home. I also looked after calves, which had to be taken for grazing for a greater part of the day. When I became older, I sometimes accompanied my father, when he was not working at the mission station, or some other adult person to graze cattle. The cattle had to be taken far from our home to where they could get fresh grass. During the dry season, they had to travel a longer distance, again in search of grass. At times, adult men had to travel so far from home with the cattle that they could not come back home in the evening. In such circumstances they erected temporary shelters and stayed in the wilderness for a considerable length of time, until there was rain and the cattle could be brought back home. At those times, women and children took food to the men in their temporary homes and got milk. We children would sometimes get a treat of being given warm milk immediately after the cows had been milked, especially from cows which had just given birth. The milk from these cows is called *umuhondo* because of the yellowish colour, and adults are not supposed to drink it.

As a child, I learnt the art of milking cows, though I must say I never became an expert. However, as a boy I was expected to learn everything concerning cattle rearing, and my father became very cross with me if I showed signs of being maladroit in dealing with cattle. He would admonish me and say I would be a good for nothing man if I did not learn the art and science of rearing cattle from a tender age. In traditional Rwanda, cattle were at the centre of the national psyche. The economy, the political system, the culture were all centred on cattle. Even today, the traditional greetings in Rwanda make reference to cattle ownership:

*Amashyo* (May you have troops of cattle); *Amashongore* (May you have female troops of cattle).

It was therefore the duty of my father to make sure I liked cattle, and that I became knowledgeable in all aspects of cattle rearing, as expected of any Rwandese boy, especially any Tutsi boy. I must say I was more interested in going to school, than in looking after cattle. I undertook all the activities related to cattle keeping as a duty, but not with any enthusiasm.

One childhood incident which I will never forget is when I got myself into trouble and was almost killed by bees. I was probably 10 or 11 years old. I had gone to fetch water with other children. Before we arrived at the stream, we discovered a beehive up on tree branches. The oldest among us decided that we should postpone our mission of fetching water and embark on getting honey from the beehive. He climbed the tree without any precaution whatsoever, and disturbed the bees. They descended on us with vengeance and we all ran for our dear lives. Unfortunately, I was the youngest among the group; my legs could not carry me fast enough. The bees attacked my whole body. As I cried, they entered my mouth, my nostrils and my ears. Breathing became difficult and I fell down writhing on the ground. After what seemed an eternity to me, a neighbour, who was grazing cattle in the vicinity, came to my rescue. He had heard me cry. He immediately cut some branches of trees with leaves and fought the bees off my body. He succeeded in clearing them off and carried me on his back to the village dispensary. My whole body was swollen; I felt as if a thousand needles were pricking my skin and my body was on fire. I had to be admitted and spent two days at the dispensary. If this man had not reached me for another five minutes or so, I would have died.

My mother was mortified. When she saw the state I was in at the dispensary, she cried a lot and believed I would die. My father just stood at my bedside, visibly shaken, but not saying a word. I don't recall if he beat me for the mischief after leaving the dispensary; he most probably did. From that day, I had a phobia for bees.

Apart from the bee incident, I used to be sick from time to time, and my parents did not know what was wrong with me. I remember one day a white doctor came to the Nyarubuye dispensary from Kibungo, the provincial headquarters. I was taken to him and he examined me and gave me some medicine. I don't know what his diagnosis was, nor do I remember the medicine given to me. What I remember is that from that time onwards I became a healthy boy. This could have been because of the medicine; it could also have been because of the psychological satisfaction that I was treated by a white doctor, (which was perceived at the time to be an honour). The most important thing is that I got well.

As a child, I participated in the informal schooling that was provided by village elders. This was in the form of *itorero*, where young boys were taught the traditional dance *guhamiriza*. Before the coming of the white people in Rwanda, itorero was in fact a form of military training and *guhamiriza* incorporated aspects of a military parade. But with the coming of the colonial administration, this institution was transformed and undertook cultural performances.

While boys were involved in *guhamiriza*, girls were taught kubyina. Unlike *guhamiriza*, *kubyina* has never been associated with military training. In pre-colonial Rwanda, girls and women probably performed these dances to entertain young men on coming home victorious from military exploits.

I started my primary education in 1955 at the age of 8 at Nyarubuye Primary School, which was not very far from our home, hardly one kilometre away. It was also part of the catholic mission. In Rwanda, as in many other African countries, western education was part and parcel of the evangelizing and colonizing project. It reminds me of the story that when the white man came to Africa, he had the Bible in one hand and a sword in the other hand. He gave Africans the Bible and told them to close their eyes and pray. When they opened their eyes, they had the Bible and the white man had the land!

For Rwanda this was predominantly the Catholic Church. White Fathers *(Pères Blancs)*, a missionary order established by Cardinal Lavigerie in 1868, had first come to Rwanda in 1900. They established the first mission station at Save near Butare in the southern part of the country that same year. The second mission was established at Zaza in the east in 1902. Nyarubuye mission station was established much later in 1939 after several other mission stations had been established. It started as a temporary grass thatched church. The permanent brick and tile church was built between 1939 and 1943. Building the church was a task that was completed through blood, sweat and tears. Apart from the bricks that were made locally, all the other materials, including heavy timber, were transported on foot, carried by men who used only their muscles, from Zaza (about 60km away) or Kabgayi (more than 200km away).

This mission school experience was at first rather strange. I was introduced to two new languages I had never come across: French and Latin. I encountered French in the classroom and Latin in the church as an altar boy. In the classroom, we would chant French words without really understanding what they meant:

*J'ai (I have)*
*Tu as (You have)*
*Il a (He has)*
*Nous avons (We have)*
*Vous avez (You have)*
*Ils ont (They have)*

In the church, as an altar boy, I would chant Latin prayers without understanding anything. I, however, enjoyed being an altar boy because, somehow, I felt I was superior to other people in the congregation. I went into the sacristy with the priest to get dressed for the occasion and would be near the priest throughout the church service. It was as if the priest and I were closer to God than the rest. I and other altar boys would even, from time to time, be naughty and taste a few drops of altar wine in the sacristy, the leftovers in the goblets after mass. Of course this would be without the knowledge of the priest.

My role as an altar boy left an indelible impression on my young mind. At that time, my ambition was to be a priest when I grew old. At home I would imagine myself as a priest and go through the motions of celebrating the holy mass, using a 'chalice' I had made from a small tin. I played this game almost every day, whenever I had the chance to do so. My mother ensured that my 'chalice' was properly kept in a safe place.

My ambition to become a priest was made even more intense because of the influence of one of the priests at the mission station, Father Vaneste. He was an old, gentle priest from Ostende in Belgium. He would call me in his office and show me illustrated books of beautiful cathedrals in Belgium: Liège, Bruges and Namur. The books also had colour pictures of white altar boys dressed in beautiful vestments. He always encouraged me to become a priest. I would then ask him whether I would be able to travel to Belgium and see all the beautiful things he was showing me if I became a priest. He would say of course I would be able to go to Belgium. At that time, visiting Europe was a dream I could never imagine would one day come true.

Another priest at the mission station was Father Giles, also a Belgian. He was flamboyant, always very smart in his white robe, with well-polished and shiny shoes. He was a chain smoker. He liked to say, jokingly, that he was from the Rwandese royal family: *"Nje ndi Semugeshi pe rwose; nje ndi umunyiginya pe rwose."* (I am Semugeshi; I am a true member of the Rwandese royal family). Later, when the White Fathers made an about turn and started supporting the Hutu against the Tutsi, he would say he was no longer a member of the Rwandese royal family; that all Belgians would, in any case, leave Rwanda to the Hutu majority and go to 'their' Congo. At that time I was probably too young to fully understand the meaning of all this talk. It was only later that I started 'seeing the light' and understood that this was the cold war being played out in public: the Tutsi were communists who wanted to throw the Belgians out of the country. They were also feudalists who wanted to keep the Hutu majority under permanent oppression. What the White Fathers did not say is that they were the ones who had indoctrinated the Tutsi to think they were superior to the Hutu in the first place.

During my childhood at Nyarubuye, the concepts of Hutu and Tutsi meant nothing to me. I played with all the children in the village, irrespective of whether they were Hutu or Tutsi. I am sure even the other children did not know or care about the difference. Now, looking back, I know that many of the children I played with were either the victims or the perpetrators of the Nyarubuye massacre in 1994. I just don't understand how human beings can change from being human and become worse than animals.

My father started working for the Catholic Church as a clerk at Nyarubuye mission in 1943. He had first been a foreman supervising the building of the mission station between 1939 and 1943, when the church building was completed. His performance as a building foreman had been so impressive that the parish priest, Father Permantien, gave him a cow as a 'handshake' for his hard and diligent work. He also built the 'European' house mentioned earlier for him. I guess being made a clerk was a promotion from being a building foreman. My father never had any formal education. He taught himself how to read and write, with the help of a few boys in the village who had had an opportunity to go to school. Sometimes he would stand behind the classroom while he was grazing calves near the school and listen to the teacher. When the children who had been inside the classroom came out, they would be surprised to find that he knew all they had learnt that day. The fact that he got the job of a clerk at the mission station is enough evidence that the White Fathers at the mission had confidence in his literacy skills. He actually had a beautiful handwriting, much better than mine. As a clerk, he was responsible for keeping all the records of the mission station: ledgers of baptism, confirmation, marriages, deaths, etc., as well as the correspondence between the mission and the diocese headquarters at Kabgayi.

What I vividly remember about my father working at the mission station is that from time to time he would bring some bread which we took for breakfast, and occasionally even a grilled chicken; gifts from the parish priest. These were treats that only a mission clerk had access to, and I am sure no one else in the village had bread for breakfast or a grilled chicken for dinner. I would, of course, make a point of announcing this to my playmates whenever such occasions – which were not very frequent – presented themselves. This added to the general belief in the village that we were a privileged family.

The other thing that I remember are the bicycle rides that my father gave me, especially on Sundays to and from church service. One day we had an accident when I put my foot in the bicycle spokes. The bicycle lost balance and we fell down. My foot was slightly injured, but otherwise we were both alright. From that time onwards, my father decided that I would sit on the crossbar in front of him, rather than on the carrier at the back. This way he would keep an eye on me. Again, a bicycle at that time was a status symbol, as not many people in the village had one.

## Zaza: The Long Walk to Education

I passed my lower primary school education (Grade 5) at Nyarubuye Primary School in 1959 and was selected to go to a boarding school at *École Normale*, Zaza, some 60 km from Nyarubuye. In those days there was no public transport at all. Therefore, at the tender age of 13 I had to walk for two days, bare foot, to Zaza. Fortunately, my elder brother Louis was already at Zaza, so we would go together, in the company of other students. Before the journey, my father would bless both of us by making the sign of the cross on our foreheads with his right thumb. The first day we would walk to Kibungo, about midway between Nyarubuye and Zaza. We would spend the night with family friends who lived in Kibungo. The following morning we would start again and arrive at Zaza in the evening. During the holidays, we would do the same thing back to Nyarubuye. Strangely, even though this was a very tiring journey and I was exhausted at the end of it, I always saw this as an adventure and I somehow enjoyed it.

Zaza was an eye opener for me. For the first time, I met children from different parts of the country. They were both Hutu and Tutsi, but again this did not mean anything to me at that time. The only difference I noticed was that some of them spoke different dialects of Kinyarwanda from mine. I found their speech rather strange, and no doubt they also found my dialect strange. But once at school, we all had to speak French only. This was a big challenge as we were not proficient enough in the language. Nevertheless, we had to make an effort. All the subjects were taught in French, except Kinyarwanda. The *École Normale* Zaza was run by Belgian *Frères de la Charité* (Brothers of Charity). It had a section of Upper Primary School (Grades 6 and 7), as well as a four year Teacher Training College. My elder brother was in the third year of the Teacher Training College when I joined Grade 6. I vividly remember some of the brothers who were teaching us. Frère Monaldi was the Rector *(Frère Supérieur)*. Frère Auxille was the musician and taught us many songs, mainly religious songs as well as songs about Belgium. We sang about the beauty of the Belgian spring without knowing even what spring is.

Frère Alliard (nicknamed Kinyundo because he was considered a cruel man by students) was the college accountant and also looked after the College farms. Frère Julien (we called him Kabuguzo because he was very short), the only Rwandese brother, taught us mathematics and geography, Belgian geography of course. I knew about the River Meuse of Belgium before I knew about the Nyabarongo, Akagera and

Akanyaru. I knew about the Ardennes Mountains before I knew about the Virunga, or even Kilimanjaro, the highest mountain in Africa. The same bias existed in the history lessons. We learnt Belgian history before we knew anything about Rwandese history. When the Canadian Head of the Frères de la Charité came to visit Zaza, we sang *"Le Canada, terre de nos aïeux"* (Canada, the land of our ancestors)!

Frère Julien had a strange way of teaching us manners. If you yawned in class without covering your mouth with your hand, he would clutch at his desk and feign to be struggling very hard, until you closed your mouth. He would then say you almost swallowed him.

Life at Zaza was not bad at all. We were well looked after. The food was good at least by my standards at that time. With hindsight, there are certain types of food we were given that I would not eat today. For example, we were served sweet potatoes with boiled palm oil as a sauce. At that time, this was fine and we actually liked it very much. Although I like sweet potatoes even today, I am not sure I would eat them in that combination. We had tea and bread with margarine spread for breakfast, which I am sure none of us would have boasted of having at home. Lunch and dinner were varied and we had plenty of fruits from the College orchards. From time to time, we had a treat of pork from Frère Alliard's pig farm. Our clothes were washed and pressed for us. You just left your dirty clothes and linen on your bed in the morning, and in the evening they were returned, clean and fresh. We were even given a *robe de nuit* (a long gown in place of pyjamas). I had my first pair of rubber shoes; this was a landmark event in my life. I had never worn any shoes before.

While I was at Zaza, Father Vaneste was transferred from Nyarubuye to Zaza because of old age. Zaza had more medical facilities than Nyarubuye, and it was also a kind of retirement centre for missionaries in that region. One morning while we were taking breakfast, the Rector came into the refectory and announced the death of Father Vaneste: *"Le Père Vaneste est mort"* he said. I was very sad. Later that day, all students at the College went to the parish church for the requiem mass. Father Vaneste was in a simple wooden open coffin. He lay there very peacefully holding a rosary in his hands. One would think that he was just asleep. It was my first time to see a dead body, let alone a white man's dead body.

The other dead body I saw at Zaza was that of a Carmelite nun who had passed away in the convent in the neighbourhood of our College. The Carmelite convent was different from other convents. It was, in fact, a kind of monastery. The nuns in the convent never left their compound.

They were enclosed in the compound for as long as they lived; their work being mainly prayer. From time to time, we at the College were allowed to go and share the holy mass with the nuns. So when one of them died, apparently from cancer, we went to pay our last respects and participated in the requiem mass.

*École Normale* Zaza was for all intents and purposes like a catholic seminary. Our daily routine always started with the holy mass in the College chapel before breakfast. A priest from the parish would come to officiate at the mass. At 12 noon and 6 pm we would again go to the chapel for a short prayer, the *Angelus*. Before we went to bed, we would have another short prayer, this time in our respective classes after preparation time (private study). On Sundays, we would go to the parish church to join the community surrounding the College for church service.

At Zaza, I was a member of the Xaverians, an organization whose activities are like those of the Boy Scouts. The main aim of the organization was to inculcate into our young minds the virtues of hard work, endurance in the face of difficulties, team work and prayer. We would, for instance, go camping outside the College for two or three days. During that time, we would sleep in tents, cook our own food and do a lot of manual work helping villagers in the neighbourhood.

It was at Zaza in early 1960 that I started understanding that those were hard times politically for Rwanda. PARMEHUTU *(Parti du Mouvement de l'Emancipation Hutu)*, the party for the emancipation of the 'Hutu nation' had put in motion a 'Hutu revolution' in 1959 soon after the death of King Mutara III Rudahigwa. He had died in Usumbura (Bujumbura) in July 1959 in suspicious circumstances. It was widely believed that he had been poisoned by the Belgians in order to give way to the Hutu revolution. PARMEHUTU was led by Grégoire Kayibanda, an ex-seminarian at Nyakibanda Major Seminary, whose mentor was Monseigneur André Perraudin, the Swiss-born Bishop of Kabgayi. I started realizing at Zaza that senior Hutu students, especially those from Gitarama, the stronghold of PARMEHUTU, were already forming small groups for political agitation.

On 30th April 1960, a group of students from Zaza travelled to Kabgayi to witness Monseigneur Perraudin being given a *pallium*. This is an ecclesiastical vestment in the Catholic Church, usually reserved for the Pope, but the Pope can allow a Bishop to wear it to signify his seniority and as a symbol of his ministry in a given area. A representative of the Pope had come all the way from the Vatican to officiate at the ceremony.

I was among the students who were selected to go to Kabgayi. We travelled by lorry on a very rough road. It was a very uncomfortable journey for me, especially as this was my first long journey in a vehicle. We had a stop-over in Kigali for lunch, and then proceeded to Kabgayi. We spent the night in a nearby school at Byimana. The *pallium* ceremony was on 1st May 1960. There were a lot of people at the ceremony from all over the country.

The Bishop was being given the *pallium* in recognition of the good work he was doing for the Catholic Church in Rwanda. However, this was not only about religious service; it was also about the political climate in the country at that time. The Catholic Church in Rwanda had very clearly shown that it sided with the Hutu project of overthrowing the monarchy and establishing a Hutu Republic. Bishop Perraudin was in the forefront of supporting this project, side by side with his political protégé, Grégoire Kayibanda. Even as the ceremony was underway, ethnic Tutsi people around Kabgayi and Gitarama were being killed, or were fleeing their homes to save their lives.

The day after the *pallium* ceremony, we went back to Zaza, the same rough ride. The rest of the year passed peacefully at the College. I passed my Grade 6 exams and was promoted to Grade 7. However, elsewhere in the country things were not good. A lot of Tutsi had been killed, especially in the central and northern parts of the country. Houses, again belonging to Tutsi, were being burnt down and owners forced to flee to neighbouring countries. Then, one fine January morning in 1961, our Kinyarwanda teacher, Mr. Venant Munyakazi, came at breakfast time and triumphantly announced to us: *"Ce qui était Lumumba est mort."* Roughly translated, he told us "The thing that was called Lumumba is dead!" Mr. Munyakazi was a Tutsi, but he was a member of PARMEHUTU. Now, looking back, I see that it was not by coincidence that it was he who came to announce Lumumba's death. Lumumba was considered a dangerous communist by the Belgians, as were Tutsi politicians in Rwanda at that time. So Lumumba's death called for celebration, but Lumumba was so feared and hated that the Belgian Brothers left it to 'his masters' voice' to announce the death of this 'dirty thing'.

Later the same year, I remember one day Frère Julien came to class unusually happy and started teaching us a song:

*La brouille loin de nous*
*Cavalier jusqu'au bout*
*Bon camarade avant tout*

[My rough translation: trouble should be far away from us; they are arrogant to the end; what we need is good people before anything else]. We happily sang the song, but were intrigued why he was teaching us that song. He was not the music teacher. It was the next day that I realized why he had taught us the song. My elder brother Louis came to me at break time and told me he was going home because he and six other students, all Tutsi, had been expelled. I went back to class crying, and it happened to be Frère Julien's geography class. He shouted at me: stop crying; *la brouil e loin de nous*, that's it! So now I knew; my brother was *la brouil* e that had to be removed from the College, lest he contaminate the good guys. I learnt later from my brother that he and his fellow students had been expelled because they were 'involved in politics'. Their involvement was simply that they clearly sided with UNAR *(Union Nationale Rwandaise)*, the party that opposed PARMEHUTU's ethnic ideology. The manifestation of their involvement in politics was singing UNAR songs, especially when outside the College campus. However, Hutu students were doing exactly the same thing, singing PARMEHUTU songs. This was, therefore, clear evidence of double standards on the part of the College authorities. What the Tutsi students did was interpreted as being involved in politics, while the same behaviour by Hutu students was condoned.

Daggers had been drawn. It was now an open secret that Hutu and Tutsi students were not on good terms. It was also clear that the College administration was siding with the Hutu students against the Tutsi 'trouble'.

Stripping people of their humanity in order to exterminate them has always been the strategy of those bent on killing with impunity: You first convince those you are indoctrinating that your adversaries are less than human beings; it is therefore justifiable to mistreat or kill them. So, calling my brother and those expelled together with him 'trouble' was part of that hate speech. These are not normal students; they are dangerous and must be removed from amongst normal human beings. That is why Lumumba was referred to as 'the thing that was called Lumumba' by Venant Munyakazi. Later on, in preparation of the genocide, the hate speech was to be perfected by Léon Mugesera, an MRND ideologue, when he called on all the Hutu people to kill Tutsi 'cockroaches' and 'snakes' and dispatch them to their 'home' in Ethiopia through the Nyabarongo River (Léon Mugesera took refuge in Canada after the genocide, but was extradited in 2013 to Rwanda to face charges of crimes against humanity.). The reference to Ethiopia stems from the belief that Tutsi people came from Ethiopia in the 15<sup>th</sup> century and found the Hutu already settled in Rwanda. Hutu extremists used this possible history as 'evidence' that the Tutsi were foreigners in Rwanda and should either be killed or sent back to Ethiopia. Who can feel guilty for killing a cockroach or a snake? In Libya, Col. Gaddafi's opponents were called rats. Ironically, it was Gaddafi himself who was killed like a rat, when he was caught hiding in a sewer! President Assad of Syria calls his opponents germs.

Just before the College was closed for the holidays, we Grade 7 pupils were required to indicate where we wanted to go for further studies in case we passed our examinations at the end of the year. We had several options. One was to continue at Zaza and do the four year teacher training programme. Alternatively, one could go to Rwesero Junior Seminary as a first stage of preparation to become a priest. The third alternative was to go to a secondary school, and hopefully later to the only tertiary institution in Rwanda at that time, the *Groupe Scolaire* at Astrida (today the National University of Rwanda, Butare).

I indicated that I wanted to go to Rwesero Junior Seminary. Arrangements were made for the Rector of the Seminary, a Belgian priest, to come and interview boys who had shown interest in joining his institution. When I went into the interview room, I was asked several questions intended to gauge my academic competence. Then there were two questions which I had not expected. I was asked whether my father was a politician and whether he was a member of UNAR. To both questions I answered truthfully and innocently that I did not know. It was later that the gravity of those two questions sank into my young mind. The Rector must have been briefed by the College authorities that I was the young brother of Louis, who had been expelled from the College recently for being 'engaged in politics' and for being a member of UNAR. Obviously the intent must have been to find out if my father was as bad as my elder brother. In the event, I never got any feedback on the outcome of the interview because, though I did not know it, my *séjour* (stay) at Zaza was coming to an end.

I left Zaza in August 1961 for the holidays. I never went back. When the College re-opened, I was already on the other side of the Rwanda-Tanganyika border – a refugee. The massacres and arson that had started in central and northern Rwanda in 1959 had now spread throughout the country. Homes belonging to Tutsi families were being burnt down, and Tutsi people were being killed by their Hutu neighbours. In eastern Rwanda (Gisaka), people did not believe that what was happening in the rest of the country would also happen to them. After all, legend had it that the *Banyanduga* (people from the central part of Rwanda) were well known for being quarrelsome and trouble makers; while the people of Gisaka were gentle and peace loving. For their part, the *Banyanduga* believed that the *Banyagisaka* were witches and could fly at night on a piece of broken pot, or light their fingers and use them as a torch at night without being burnt!

It was in the middle of 1961 that arson and killings spread to Gisaka, so when I went back home in August 1961 there was trouble in my childhood paradise.

Nyarubuye, Rwanda (2013): Nyarubuye Roman Catholic Church

Nyarubuye, Rwanda (1996): Aloys Rubagumya (1916–1997)

# Chapter Two

# The Forest, Karagwe and Beyond

## Refuge in the Forest

Hutu agitators had already started mobilizing people on the hills surrounding Nyarubuye, urging them to start burning homes that belonged to Tutsi villagers. For several days many Tutsi families took refuge at Nyarubuye mission station. During this time, my family remained at home. For some reason, my father must have believed that nothing would happen to us. Then one day, we heard that an old man, probably over 80 years old, had been killed on the orders of the local *Bourgmestre*. It was alleged that the old man had been hiding his son, who was wanted by the local Hutu authorities.

That was the signal that many people were waiting for. There was now no doubt in anybody's mind that war had come to Nyarubuye. My father decided in consultation with close relatives in the area that we had to flee to Tanganyika (to become Tanzania later in 1964). The Rwanda-Tanganyika border nearest our village was the Kagera River, a few kilometres east of Nyarubuye. We gathered a few belongings, mainly clothes, bedding and whatever food provisions we could carry. As it happened, the decision to go into exile at that particular time was a wise one because, we were told later, just one day after our departure soldiers came to our home looking for my father and my elder brother. Had we not left on that day, I think I would be telling a different story.

We started walking towards the Kagera River. The men took care of the cattle, while the women and children carried the belongings. Some of our Hutu neighbours escorted us to the border and assured us that they had nothing against us. With hindsight, maybe some of them were silently rejoicing, planning to take over our property. Our property was in fact not taken over because my paternal grandmother and one cousin of mine remained behind. My grandmother was too old to go into exile, and my cousin decided he would not leave her alone. As things turned out, my grandmother died of old age two years after our departure and my cousin remained in Rwanda. He died of natural causes at Nyarubuye after the genocide. I, however, think that our neighbours were good people; otherwise they would have killed us.

Once at the river bank, negotiations started with owners of dug-out canoes to facilitate our crossing the river to safety on the other side of the border. Crossing the river was a bit tricky. We were six families with a total of about 30 people and around forty head of cattle. Whereas the canoe could carry three to four people at a time, two men in a canoe could manoeuvre only one cow across at a time. While one canoe operator rowed the canoe, the second led the cow using a strong rope tied around its neck. One by one, the cattle swam across the river, guided by the man holding the rope from inside the canoe. After several hours, this precarious operation was over and we were all safe on the Tanganyika side of the border. We camped at the river bank for one night. The following morning we had to move further from the border. This was a forest area, with no people living in the vicinity. The roaring of lions that night was a very frightening experience indeed.

We set up camp a few kilometres from the river, with very rudimentary living conditions. A few thatched huts were built by men. On a piece of land, trees were cut down and were used to build the huts. These huts were built close to each other for security reasons, in view of wild animals, especially lions, in the area. Another security precaution was to light a fire at night to scare animals away. We lived as one community, rather than as separate families. Men and boys were assigned a few huts, as were women and girls. Cooking was done communally in the open.

The food consisted mainly of beans with *ugali* made of millet flour. We also shared whatever little milk there was. At night, men would sneak across the river back into Rwanda in order to get food provisions as there was no food anywhere near our camp. Obviously, this was a very risky undertaking on two counts. They risked being captured and probably killed inside Rwanda. They also risked being attacked by wild animals in the forest.

One day, about three weeks after we had crossed into Tanganyika, my father crossed back into Rwanda when we were told that the situation was now calm. He wanted to find out for himself whether we could go back home. We had not resigned ourselves to being refugees for ever. In fact all the adults in the camp believed this situation was temporary and that very soon we would all go back home. When my father reached Nyarubuye, he went straight to the mission station and met Father Van Lier, the Belgian priest in charge of the mission station. Father Van Lier told my father that he could go back to his job as a clerk and that I could go back to school at *École Normale*, Zaza. When my father asked Father Van Lier if he thought the war was over, he was told that the war was over for the time being, but the next round would be even more deadly. The next morning, my father crossed the border back to Tanganyika, determined to make the best of a difficult situation for his family. Father Van Lier must have known what he was talking about. Since there was no question of our going back to Rwanda any time soon, the plan was now to move from the forest to Karagwe. The decision was made by my father, because he was the oldest man in the group, and all in the group were actually related. So everybody looked up to my father as the natural leader of the group.

Fortunately, I spent only a few weeks in this wilderness. My father arranged for me and one of my cousins, Noel Bulamba, to go to Karagwe in order to continue with our education. We were to go and stay with our uncle, Venant Bagirishya. Our uncle had moved to Karagwe many years before and he was well established. He was also well connected because his sister had married the *Omukama* (Chief) of Karagwe, Bernard Itogo Ruhinda. One day, our uncle came to take us. We walked a few kilometres to the nearest road and boarded a bus to Karagwe.

I left with a heavy heart. First because I was leaving my parents and going to live with somebody I did not know. Secondly, I left my young sister Irene behind in the forest. She had completed her Grade 4 before we crossed the border and she had been doing very well at school.

My father decided that there was no point for a girl to go to school in the circumstances. She was therefore to stay behind, and that was it. Nobody in the family could contradict his decision. This was a defining moment for me and my sister. I had been given the opportunity to go to school, and she was denied it simply because she was a girl. This was patriarchy at its worst. Today, my sister is a peasant farmer in Kirehe District, in eastern Rwanda. The different paths of her life opportunities and mine were determined by my father's decision to deny her a chance to continue with her education. To be fair to my father, everybody probably expected him to make this choice given the circumstances; and he was not the only one to make such a decision.

## A New Beginning in Karagwe

We arrived in Karagwe exhausted from the long bus ride. The topography of Karagwe was not very different from that of eastern Rwanda: the same undulating hills, the same banana groves covering the hills and valleys; it was as if I was going back to Nyarubuye.

My cousin and I settled very easily in our new family. We met new relatives we did not know before. One of the first challenges we encountered was a linguistic one. Apart from our uncle, no one else spoke Kinyarwanda or French. Everybody spoke either Kinyambo, which is the local language in Karagwe, or Kiswahili. Of course we did not speak either language. When we were taken to a local primary school a few days after our arrival, things became even more complicated because there was another new language, English. It is surprising how quickly we acclimatized to the new environment. Within a few weeks we could already communicate fairly effectively with fellow pupils in either Kinyambo or Kiswahili. English took a bit longer, but after a couple of months we were actually better in English than the pupils we had found at the school. Part of the reason for this might be because we had actually completed primary school (seven years) in Rwanda before coming to Karagwe, and we were now admitted into Grade Five. We were actually supposed to start secondary school. Having learnt some French must have also helped us to learn English much faster. Maybe more importantly, we had to learn to communicate with people around us, and this was the case for all three languages: Kinyambo, Kiswahili and English.

1962 was a bit unsettled because we attended two different schools. We first went to Ihembe Primary School, near our uncle's home. Later in the year we were transferred to Nyaishozi Middle School because Ihembe's level of education was too low for us, language problems notwithstanding. At Nyaishozi we were enrolled into Grade Six. In 1963 we moved yet to another school, Lukajange Middle School, where we entered Grade Seven. While at Nyaishozi, we stayed with another uncle, Ananias Bizima. By this time our parents had also moved to Karagwe from the wilderness, so when we moved to Lukajange we could stay with them while attending school.

When the rest of my family came to Karagwe from the forest, they were received by a local man called Selemani Rushagama, who was the husband of my maternal aunt, Zenobia. He and my aunt Zenobia lived at Kayanga Village, not very far from the District Headquarters. My parents were given a house to stay in and a sizeable banana grove. All they had to do is to tend the grove and to plant other food crops like beans, maize and vegetables. This was not a bad beginning, compared to other refugees who had to go into refugee camps and depend on food hand-outs from the UNHCR, at least for the first few months of their arrival in Tanganyika. In short, we were given an opportunity to be integrated into the local community, thanks to our host Mr. Rushagama.

My recollections of visits to Mr. Rushagama's home are those of being served very hot meals, usually beef or fish stew with cooked bananas. The meals were served on a very big round dish called *sinia*. Everybody in the family would sit on the floor around the *sinia* after washing their hands and would start attacking the food from all sides. The etiquette was that you eat the food in front of you; you especially do not take a piece of beef or fish that is in front of somebody else. After the meal, we would normally get a big mug of 'tea', which was in fact boiled milk with lots of sugar.

The *Omukama* (Chief) of Karagwe, Bernard Itogo Ruhinda, married to my paternal aunt, also welcomed our family. Sometimes I would pay a visit to my aunt and stay for a couple of days at the Chief's compound at Nyakahanga Village, learning Kiswahili and English from my cousins. The Chief also gave some assistance to my family in terms of foodstuffs. Despite this relatively good beginning, life was not easy. On several occasions we had to work for our neighbours – weeding their farms – in order to get food. A whole day's work earned you a bunch of bananas and maybe a few measures of beans, which would be enough food for two or three days.

By the time we moved to Lukajange, my cousin Noel and I were very comfortable in both Kiswahili and English, at least as comfortable as anybody else at that level of education. But moving to and from school was a challenge as we lived about 10 kilometres away from the school. We had to wake up very early in the morning to walk the 10 kilometres to be on time at 8 o'clock. In the evening we had to cover the same distance back home. Fortunately, the school provided lunch.

The two years I spent at Lukajange Middle School were very important for consolidating my Kiswahili and English proficiency. I actually think I had an advantage over other pupils because I knew a bit of French. I could transfer the same skills I had used to learn French to the new situation of learning English. To give an idea of my level, some of the teachers asked me to write notes on the blackboard for other pupils to copy because they believed I would make very few mistakes, if any.

The Headteacher of Lukajange Middle School, Mr. Jonas Mugangala, was a jovial man and he always encouraged us to study hard and be like him. He had a car, a blue Volkswagen, which was a real status symbol at that time. Apart from him, the other person who had a car in Karagwe was *Omukama* (Chief) Ruhinda. So when Mr. Mugangala told us to study hard and be like him we all listened. The other teachers I liked were those who taught us English, history and geography. I did not like the mathematics teacher because I did not like mathematics. Ironically, this mathematics teacher, Mr. Elisa Lwakatare, became a good friend of mine in later years. We met again in Dar es Salaam, when he worked at the Ministry of Education Headquarters while I was at the University of Dar es Salaam. All the punishments he had given me for not completing my mathematics assignments or for scoring low marks had been forgotten and forgiven on both sides.

Lukajange was a Lutheran School. So, even though I am Catholic, I had to attend Lutheran services. Even Muslim pupils had to attend these church services. This was no problem at all for me. In fact I liked the church services, especially the songs.

While at Lukajange, fresh outbursts of violence shook Rwanda. There had been intermittent skirmishes between the Rwandese Army and Tutsi guerrilla fighters, especially those crossing from Burundi in the south. These usually moved at night so as not to be easily detected by the Rwandese army. For this reason they were called *inyenzi* (cockroaches) by the Rwandese government. In December 1963, a group of Tutsi fighters entered Rwanda from Burundi and moved north towards Kigali. They were intercepted by the army and about 14,000 of them were killed. This battle led to another round of violence within Rwanda (Prunier 1994). Tutsis who had not fled the country in 1959-1961 were persecuted by the government. They were accused of being ibyitso (collaborators) of the Tutsi invaders from Burundi. For those of us outside the country, this was another indication that we were not about to return home. We might just as well settle down where we were.

## A Tanzanian Education at Nyakato Secondary School

After two years at Lukajange Middle School, I was selected to go to Nyakato Secondary School, having passed the national Primary School Leaving Examination (Grade 8 at that time). Nyakato was, and still is, a boys' boarding school near Bukoba town, the headquarters of the West Lake Region (later to be called the Kagera Region). We were given instructions for joining the school, as well as travel warrants that allowed us to board local buses without having to pay cash. This arrangement between the government and transport operators allowed someone to travel by producing a government guarantee that the transport operator would be paid at a later date.

At Nyakato, I met other boys from different parts of West Lake Region and even a few from outside the Region. We had teachers from different countries: Britain, Germany, India, USA and, of course, Tanzania. Our physics teacher, Mr. Patel, was from India. At first it was very difficult to understand him because of his accent, but later we got used to him and we could clearly follow what he was teaching. The accent of Peace Corps volunteers from the USA was also challenging at the beginning. Mr. Scheven, our biology teacher, was from Germany. He was always very meticulous in whatever he did, and he would be very angry if he found anything in the classroom or in the biology laboratory dirty or not in its proper place. For some reason, he hated our Kiswahili teacher, Mr. Kiimbila, and he openly said it. One day he told us in his guttural German accent: *you know boyj, in zis school I hate Mr. Kiimbila and Mr. Bennett's dog.* Mr. Bennett was a geography teacher from Britain and he had a very ugly dog. Why Mr. Scheven associated Mr. Kiimbila with Mr. Bennett's dog was not clear to us. Was this some kind of a racist insult, suggesting that Mr. Kiimbila, an African teacher, was no different than a white man's dog?

The Headmaster, Mr. Phumbwe, was a graduate in history from the University College of Swansea in Wales. He was a strict disciplinarian and it was rumoured that he had been brought to Nyakato to restore discipline because Nyakato was known for indiscipline. In this task he was helped by Mr. Kiimbila, the Discipline Master. Many students disliked Mr. Kiimbila because of his harsh punishments, especially caning. He earned the nickname of Michelin (after the trade mark of Michelin tyres), because he was short and fat.

The indiscipline of students at Nyakato Secondary School was part of the school culture. For instance, Form One students were bullied by continuing students. They were called Wagogo. Wagogo are an ethnic group in central Tanzania, and Haya boys called newcomers "wagogo" because they believed Wagogo were not 'civilised'. In extreme cases, some newcomers were beaten up by older boys. This was one of the issues the Discipline Master and the Headmaster had to deal with. The other discipline problems had to do with students who went to town without permission, drunken behaviour and many such problems as would be expected of teenagers.

For the first time since leaving Rwanda, I was subjected to discrimination and harassment, especially by Haya boys. The Haya ethnic group was predominant at Nyakato, and they somehow felt superior to boys from other parts of the region, especially those from Ngara District, who were derogatively called *abashuti*. This was an insulting term reserved for people from Ngara, Rwanda and Burundi. The explanation for this behaviour can only be ethnic bigotry. Since most boys knew that I was from Rwanda, I was also referred to as *omushuti*. The etymological origin of the word *omushuti* is the Kinyarwanda word *inshuti*, which means a friend. The Haya turned this meaning upside down, using the word to identify "a worthless person; despicable, contemptible; abominable; hateful, loathsome" (Muzale 2006). At first, I would be very angry when insulted like this, but over time I decided to ignore such insults. I must say that very few boys insulted me. The majority of them were very friendly and they did not care where I came from; we were just school mates or class mates.

While at Nyakato, new far reaching developments were taking place in the educational system of Tanzania. In 1966, while I was in Form Two, University of Dar es Salaam students went on strike because they did not support National Service, which had just been introduced. According to this new policy, university graduates were supposed to serve two years as their contribution to nation building: National Service was defined as six months of military training and 18 months of working at 40% of salary. This policy caused an uproar and some students went as far as saying colonial times were better. President Nyerere was extremely upset and he charged like an angry buffalo. Students who were demonstrating in town were rounded up and taken to *Ikulu* (State House) on his orders. In the meeting, they read the speech they had prepared to argue that the proposed national service was unfair to graduates. In reply, President Nyerere started calmly and talked to them without a prepared speech. He said he agreed with them that political leaders' salaries were too big. He ordered the Minister of Finance on the spot to reduce the President's salary and that of all the Ministers by 20%. As he proceeded in his speech, he became angrier and angrier at the students for their lack of patriotism, until he reached his crescendo and told them: Go home. They thought he was telling them to go back to the University. Outside the gates of *Ikulu*, buses were waiting for them to take them back to their villages! The University was closed and all university students were sent home (Shivji 2012). For Nyerere, this meeting was evidence, if he needed any, that the education given to young people in the country was inappropriate. It was too elitist.

In 1967, partly in reaction to this university crisis, the *Arusha Declaration on Socialism and Self-reliance* was unveiled. This was Tanzania's blueprint for a socialist ideology that was to guide the country's political and socio-economic path. Along with the *Arusha Declaration* came Mwalimu Nyerere's philosophy of *Education for Self-Reliance*. Briefly put, this new philosophy was intended to do away with elitist education. Henceforth, each level of education was to prepare young men and women to be self-reliant and to prepare themselves for life in rural Tanzania, where the majority of these would eventually live. In practice, this translated in students not only learning theoretical knowledge, but also doing practical work like farming at school. In this way, their theoretical knowledge would be translated into practical skills that would help them later in life. Primary education was now supposed to be complete in itself, not a stepping stone to secondary education. The logic was that for a long time to come, Tanzania would not afford secondary education for everybody, but it could afford a good primary education for all. This education, the argument went, should prepare primary school leavers to be productive self-reliant young men and women in a socialist rural Tanzania. The same argument went for secondary education for those few who would be able to go to secondary school. In conformity with the new educational philosophy, every school in Tanzania was expected to engage students in productive work. For most schools this was translated into a school farm, where students would spend part of the school day. So in my last two years at Nyakato, we had a small banana farm. The school time table was changed in order to accommodate this new activity. However, farming was seen as an appendage to the core business of the school, which was academic lessons. In this sense, Mwalimu Nyerere's philosophy was not really understood. His idea was to have a farm, or any other economic activity at the school, as an integral part of school learning. Theoretical knowledge was supposed to be integrated with practical knowledge.

Those of us who got an opportunity to get secondary education had an extra responsibility. Mwalimu Nyerere reminded us that we were like a person sent by a starving village to go on a long journey and search for food. The villagers expect that person to find food and bring it back to the village. If this person gets food and keeps it for himself, he is a traitor. As secondary school students in those days, we were constantly reminded of this responsibility. We were not getting an education just for ourselves; the society expected a lot from us. The country was investing a lot in our education, expecting that we would, after getting that education, be in the forefront of transforming the society in which we live.

Being taught by teachers from different countries expanded our horizon and made us more broad-minded than we would otherwise have been. Moreover, interaction within the student community also played a positive role in our educational development. It was at Nyakato that I became interested in current affairs and started listening to the radio. We had one set which was switched on at certain times of the day, especially after lunch and after dinner. Senior students had a big influence on us as well. I remember particularly people like Jenerali Ulimwengu (at that time his name was Twaha Khalfan), who was two years ahead of me. He was very knowledgeable and we all wanted to be near him and listen to what he had to say.

I also developed an interest in the debating club and I eventually became president of the club while I was in Form Four. Debates were taken very seriously and people had to go to the library to prepare themselves for a debating session, especially if they were the main speakers for or against the motion. The president had a special black robe which he wore when presiding over debates. Topical issues at that time included the *Rhodesian Unilateral Declaration of Independence* (UDI), the Apartheid regime of South Africa, the *Arusha Declaration* and its implications for the development of Tanzania, and many others. Looking back, students at that time knew quite a lot of things about what was going on in the world. We took keen interest in those issues despite the fact that we had very limited access to the mass media. In Form One and Two, I was fascinated by new subjects: chemistry, physics and biology, and I indeed performed very well in those subjects. However, I did not like mathematics and, needless to say, I performed poorly in that subject. At the end of Form Two we had to choose whether to enter a science or arts stream. Because of my poor performance in mathematics, I entered the arts stream. I had, therefore, to drop chemistry and physics, and take English literature instead. Biology and mathematics were compulsory for everybody, so there was no escape for me as far as mathematics was concerned. I had to carry that cross for another two years.

I started developing interest in languages at Nyakato. We were introduced to the works of Shakespeare in Form Three in the literature course. I also read a lot of novels, written by European as well as African authors. Chinua Achebe's *Things Fal Apart* was my favourite novel. It was very easy to connect to because its cultural context was not very unfamiliar. However, even novels written by Europeans were not entirely irrelevant. They actually sharpened one's imagination with unfamiliar contexts. Shakespeare's plays were very difficult at first, but once introduced by the teacher they became very enjoyable. The themes covered by Shakespeare are about universal human experience, irrespective of what culture one comes from.

We were encouraged to practice our English through a number of activities, including debates, writing letters to pen pals in different parts of the world (I remember I had pen pals from the USA and Australia), and participating in essay competitions. When I was in Form Three, I won the East African Brooke Bond essay competition and was awarded *The Complete Works of Shakespeare*.

At Nyakato, life was not easy for me. Of course all the basics of life were provided. But as the Bible says, 'man does not live on bread alone'!

I was from a poor refugee family, so I did not have pocket money even for very small needs. This troubled me, because some of my classmates were relatively better off and naturally I felt bad when I could not afford the things they were buying. My solution was to ask for some menial jobs from my teachers, like cutting grass around their houses. American teachers were very generous. I usually got these petty jobs over the weekend when I was free. I would be given one or two shillings for a two hour job. That was a lot of money as far as I was concerned.

At the end of Form Four in 1968, I got the best student's prize in the Arts stream. On the basis of mock examinations, I was pre-selected to join Mzumbe Secondary School in Morogoro for Forms Five and Six. At that time, examinations were set and marked by the Cambridge Examinations Syndicate. Those selected to go to Form Five on the basis of mock examination results would continue only if they passed the Cambridge School certificate examinations.

My four years at Nyakato had consolidated my integration into the Tanzanian society. The most important thing that I took from Nyakato was Nyerere's idea that education is not for personal gain; it should be for the service of humanity.

By the time I completed Form Four, Rwanda was becoming more distant in terms of the possibility of going back. Nyakato also improved my language skills in Kiswahili and English. The French I had learnt in Rwanda was becoming more dysfunctional as days went by, because I had no opportunity of using it. As I prepared to go to Mzumbe, I felt I was going even further away from Rwanda, both geographically and emotionally.

Nyakato, Tanzania (1966): The author in Form Two, Nyakato Secondary School.

## Foundering at Mzumbe Secondary School

In January 1969, I joined Mzumbe Secondary School. We boarded the steamer, *MV Victoria*, and travelled over night to Mwanza. This was my first experience of travelling on a steamer. The journey was very uncomfortable because the third class compartment was full of people. There was hardly any space to sit comfortably, let alone get some sleep. I was worried I would throw up if the lake got rough, but fortunately it was calm all the way to Mwanza. In fact, while inside the steamer, I didn't even realise it was moving; it was as if we were just seated there going nowhere.

From Mwanza we boarded the train to Morogoro. Again this was my first experience on a train. At Mwanza railway station, I marvelled at the long iron snake which I was about to board. Travelling to Morogoro was a good lesson in endurance. The train was even more uncomfortable than the steamer, again because the third class coaches were steaming with people. At night it was impossible to sleep. The whole journey from my home in Karagwe to Morogoro took about 72 hours non-stop by bus, steamer and train. It was also a good lesson in the topographical features of the country, at least for those parts of the journey which were covered during daylight. I could experience first-hand what I had learnt in geography, for instance, about the *miombo* woodlands in central Tanzania. I marvelled at the mango trees in the Tabora region. I just wondered whether these were planted by human beings or whether they just grew naturally. Crossing the Great Rift Valley by train was an exhilarating experience, going down the valley and up. Along the railway line, at each station, there were people selling all sorts of foodstuffs to passengers: barbecue chicken, boiled maize, eggs, you name it. It was rumoured that what looked like chicken was in fact wild birds. However, that did not deter people from buying the meat.

Form Five was a class of 25 students from all over the country. This was a pioneer class, being the first Form Five intake. Hitherto there had been only up to Form Four. I was to take English literature, history and geography. Being a pioneer class had its teething problems. For one thing, the library was not equipped with the necessary books for 'A' levels. Fortunately we were very close to the Institute of Development Management (IDM) Mzumbe. Special arrangements were made for us to use their library, and this access made a big difference.

At Mzumbe Secondary School, my horizon was further broadened, not only by more advanced studies, but also by the exposure to more people from different corners of the country. Compared to Mzumbe, Nyakato had been more parochial in the sense that the majority of students were from the West Lake Region (today Kagera Region). Mzumbe was more national in character, and I believe this was good for me in terms of seeing the bigger picture. The majority of staff were Tanzanians, but we had one Indian, Mr. Patel (no relation to Mr. Patel of Nyakato Secondary School), Mr. Kirk, an Irishman, and one African-American, Mrs. Enyi, who was married to a Nigerian professor teaching at Morogoro Agricultural College (now Sokoine University of Agriculture).

Mr. Patel taught us European history. He had a red Mercedes Benz car which he called the red elephant. He was rather good at blowing his own trumpet; he thought he was the best teacher, and he always reminded us that the best teacher is the one who does not teach. At first we did not understand him, but later we realized that he was probably right. The best teacher is the one who does not spoon feed his students; rather he guides them to learn. Our other history teachers were Mr. Makubi and Mr. Mabugo. Mr. Makubi taught us 'World Affairs since 1945' while Mr. Mabugo taught us African history, which I particularly liked.

African literature was taught by Mr. Kirk. I particularly remember one of the set books we used for African literature, *A Grain of Wheat* by Ngũgĩ wa Thiong'o. This novel is about sacrifice and betrayal. As I look at what is happening in Tanzania and many other African countries today, I remember the novel. There are leaders in Africa who sacrificed everything, including their lives, for the emancipation of Africa. However, subsequent generations of leaders have not necessarily been faithful to the ideals of the founding fathers of African nations. There has, therefore, been betrayal of these ideals. Although *A Grain of Wheat* is about Kenya, it is relevant to many African countries.

Mrs. Enyi taught us literature in English, but by non-African writers. I had a bit of a problem with her. At Mzumbe I was very slim and rather frail. Mrs. Enyi took every opportunity to remind me of this, as if I needed reminding. When we were in Form Six, one day in class we were discussing one character in a novel, a boy who couldn't defend himself when he was bullied by other boys. I think the novel was D.H. Laurence's *Sons and Lovers*. Mrs. Enyi asked me if I could box. I said I couldn't. Then with a mocking smile she said, "with all due respect to Casmir, what kind of a man cannot box?" That was the proverbial last straw that broke the camel's back. I was so furious that I retorted, "Mrs. Enyi, with all due respect, this is not a boxing academy". I immediately stormed out of the class. The next morning she called me to her office and apologized. She said she had not meant to humiliate me in front of my classmates. However, the damage had already been done. From that day onwards, I did attend her classes, but I was so put off by her presence that I could not really concentrate on what she was teaching. That cost me dearly, because I could not get a principal pass in literature in my Advanced Level school certificate examinations. I strongly suspect that out of the three papers in literature it was her paper that I failed.

At Mzumbe I had very low morale. Mrs. Enyi contributed to this, but she was not the only reason for my feeling low. It would be unfair to attribute all my problems at Mzumbe to her. The main reason, I think, was that I now realized I was coming to the end of my secondary education with no clear idea as to what would happen next. I was still a refugee, and my home country, Rwanda, was still a faraway dream. There was no hope of going back any time soon.

Despite feeling low, there were some moments of cheerfulness all the same. I was involved in the school magazine, for which I was Editor-in-Chief when I was in Form Six, and my interest in debating was still intact. We had a lot of debating sessions, both within the school and outside the school. We were, for example, invited to debate with students at Kilakara Girls Secondary School in Morogoro. We also had opportunities to go outside Morogoro. We visited Mazengo Secondary School and Msalato Secondary School, both in Dodoma, as well as Tanga Secondary School.

Apart from debating trips, we also had other academic excursions. I remember vividly the trip our class had to Dar es Salaam to visit the National Museum, as well as the trip to Bagamoyo to visit places of historical interest: the old slave market, the first Catholic Church in Tanzania, as well as the Kaole Ruins. This trip meant a lot to me. I was, in fact, learning something about African history for the first time in my life. As mentioned earlier, in Rwanda I had only learnt about Belgian history, as if Rwanda did not have a history. The trip, especially the visit to the Catholic Church, reminded me of Nyarubuye Catholic Church, but also evoked thoughts of the role of the church in Rwanda politics.

One of the challenges of being a refugee was not having money for unexpected expenses. While at Mzumbe Secondary School, I think I was in Form Five, I started having problems with my eye sight. The school doctor referred me to Morogoro Regional Hospital. I had my eyes examined, and the eye specialist recommended that I buy eye glasses. I reported back to the school doctor, who in turn recommended that I go to Dar es Salaam to make the purchase. I went to the Second Master to ask for permission to travel to Dar es Salaam for that purpose, but also to ask for financial assistance. The Second Master did not have any problem giving me permission to travel, but he categorically said the school was not in a position to pay for the glasses.

Fortunately, a gentleman by the name of Berchmas Gashikazi, who worked with East African Railways at a railway station near Morogoro town, was married to my cousin. I went to him and told him about my problem. Mr. Gashikazi was a very generous man. He had already supported me financially on several occasions without even my asking. When I told him I needed spectacles, he did not hesitate. He bought me a return train ticket to Dar es Salaam and gave me eighty shillings.

I boarded the train to Dar es Salaam very early in the morning. My plan had been to make a day trip to Dar es Salaam. I did not know anybody in Dar es Salaam. It was my first time to visit the city. I did not have any money to spend the night in a guest house, and I would probably have found it difficult to locate one even if I had the money! When I arrived in Dar es Salaam, I went straight to the shop recommended by the eye specialist in Morogoro. It was Kayzar's along Independence Avenue (today Samora Avenue). This was very convenient because it was near the railway station. I paid seventy shillings and remained with ten shillings.

Unfortunately, by the time I was through with my business, it was too late to go back to Morogoro by train. I therefore had to spend the night in Dar es Salaam. The hour of reckoning had come. Where would I spend the night? I still had ten shillings in my pocket, but I was not sure if I could get a safe place to stay overnight with that amount. I decided it would be safer and more convenient to spend the night at the railway station. I was not the only stranded passenger; there were quite a number of others as well. At least I had some money to buy food. I don't think I spent more than five shillings, so I actually had a surplus of five shillings when I boarded the train back to Morogoro the next morning. That was more than enough for the fare from Morogoro town to Mzumbe.

Another challenge was being excluded from activities meant for Tanzanians because I was not a citizen. At the end of Form Six, all my fellow classmates were supposed to go for National Service for a period of six months. I was not allowed to go because I was not a Tanzanian. I was therefore left in limbo, to fend for myself. This really hurt me, not necessarily because I was so keen on military training, but because of the message being conveyed to me: you are not one of us.

I started looking for temporary employment while waiting for Form Six examination results. Fortunately, towards the end of January 1971, I found a job as a temporary teacher at St. Peter's Seminary, Morogoro. I was assigned to teach history.

When the Form Six examination results were published in March 1971, they came as a big shock to me. I had scored one principal pass in History (at grade C) and subsidiary passes in Geography and Literature as well as General Paper. What this meant was that I had not passed all the papers in Geography and Literature. As I said above, I strongly suspect I had failed Mrs. Enyi's paper in Literature. I also think I probably failed the Physical Geography paper. So, apart from the challenge of being a refugee, I had now an extra challenge of trying to get access to higher education with rather poor Form Six results. However, I was determined. Mzumbe was a bad chapter in my academic life and there was no point trying to make excuses; I swore to myself that I would somehow get it behind me and move on.

By this time I was already 24 years old. Had I not got a temporary job, I would probably have gone back to the village in Karagwe. Of course for Tanzanians even those who had not passed well were assured of at least direct employment by the government. In those days, no Form Six graduate would fail to find a job if they wanted. However, even getting a temporary job was just that; a temporary solution. My future hung in the balance. Many refugees of my age, if they did not have any education, were peasants in refugee settlements or they had gone to town to try their luck at getting menial jobs. Many of my age-mates were married.

Mzumbe, Tanzania (1970): The author (standing third right) with some classmates, Form Six Mzumbe Secondary School.

# Chapter Three

# Learning to be a Teacher

## Learning to be a Teacher at St. Peter's Seminary

St. Peter's was a new experience. First, I was thrown into a teaching job
without any preparation at all. I had no professional training as a
teacher. All I had was the school knowledge I had acquired at secondary
school. Now here I was, with the responsibility of teaching History
in Forms Three and Four. Fortunately, both the management of the
seminary and the students were very supportive. Being a seminary, the
students were disciplined and highly motivated learners. I therefore did
not face any discipline problems. Again, because I was not very much
older than them, they could very easily approach me and confide in me
in a way they could not with the older teachers, especially the priests.
Looking back, I am happy to say that every time I meet a former student
from St. Peter's Seminary, I am showered with praise that I am a very
good teacher, and that they really enjoyed my history classes.

The second challenge I faced was to start being independent. I had
to start making decisions about my life without depending on anyone. I
was old enough to look after myself. As mentioned above, many of my
age-mates in the village already had families of their own. Yes, it is true
I had parents, but they were far away in Karagwe. In fact, when they
learnt that I had a job, they were now expecting me to support them
financially. For the first time in my life, I had to start thinking about how
I would get food, clothes and other necessities of life.

My salary at St. Peter's Seminary was Tanzanian shillings 550 a month
(approximately US$ 100). At that time, this was quite sufficient. I could
buy food, clothes and have a bit of savings. Fortunately, I did not have
to pay rent. I was given a house, which I shared with two other teachers,
who were also bachelors. To give an indication of the cost of living at
that time, I was able to buy my first watch for 100 shillings, and that was
an Oris watch, a very good quality Swiss brand in those days. I had the
watch until 1993, more than twenty years. I had to learn how to manage
my finances, because whatever little money I got was not just to be spent
on enjoying life; I had plans for further education. I saved every cent
possible for that purpose.

I learnt a great deal from interactions with my colleagues. When I joinedSt.Peter'sSeminaryasatemporaryteacher,therewerethreepriests. Father Emmanuel Makala was the Rector, Father Canute Mzuanda was the Bursar, and Father Walter Damen from the Netherlands was just an ordinary teacher. He had earned himself the nickname of "Butcher" from the students because, rightly or wrongly, they thought he was a cruel man. Personally, I saw no evidence that would justify such a name, but of course I was not a student. There were other lay teachers like me. Jerome Brito from India taught physics. Before meeting Mr. Brito, I did not know that there were Catholics in India. He told me that he was from Goa and that most people from that part of India were Catholics because they had been colonized by the Portuguese. Mr. Brito lived on *chapatis* and vegetables, even though his religion did not prevent him from eating meat. I tried to learn how to prepare *chapatis* from him, but I failed miserably.

There were two young women from Britain, Tess and Clare, who taught English. Sometimes they had heated arguments with me because they took exception to the way I taught South African History. Students would tell them that the British were oppressing black South Africans, and that they had learnt that from me in the history class. The two ladies would then come to me, protesting that I was distorting history, that the British had nothing to do with Apartheid in South Africa. I would retort that most white South Africans were either of British or Dutch origin. I would concede their argument that South Africans of British origin were not British citizens. I would, however, remind them that Britain was investing a lot in South Africa, and therefore the British were partly responsible for the ills of the Apartheid regime. Of course they did not accept that argument, though they could not refute it. In the end, we agreed to disagree, but remained good friends.

There were also two African-Americans on the staff of the seminary. One of them was married, and his wife was always clean shaven, no hair at all on her head. Her husband said this style was a sign of mourning for mother Africa. They had sworn that she would only grow her hair when the whole of Africa was free. They left the seminary a short time after my arrival, so I don't know how long they kept that oath.

My closest friends at the seminary were Willibald Gonda, Augustine Rudakubana and his younger brother, Callixte Kananura. All three were also temporary teachers at the seminary. Augustine and Callixte were actually refugees from Rwanda like me; they had also completed their Form Six, the former at Mazengo Secondary School and the latter at

Kibaha Secondary School. We lived in the same refugee settlement in Karagwe and knew each other before St. Peter's. Willibald had been training for the priesthood, but dropped out of Kipalapala Major Seminary. Of the three, I have kept in touch with Willibald. Callixte is dead, and his brother Augustine has since moved back to Rwanda.

While at St. Peter's, I started applying for scholarships for further study. Because of my refugee status, all my applications had to go through the office of the United Nations High Commission for Refugees (UNHCR) in Dar es Salaam.

I also made private initiatives without going through the UNHCR. For example, Mr. Gashikazi, my benefactor who had bought spectacles for me while I was at Mzumbe Secondary School, advised me to apply for a clerical training post with East African Railways. I did apply and was called for an interview in Nairobi, the headquarters of East African Railways. I was given a second class return train ticket to Nairobi. The journey to Nairobi and back was very comfortable, because with a second class ticket I could sleep at night. I could also have meals in the restaurant car of the train. In Nairobi, I met other candidates from Kenya, Uganda and Tanzania. After the interview, I went back to Morogoro to wait for the results. To be frank, I had accepted the advice to go to Nairobi just to please my benefactor. I could not imagine myself a railway clerk issuing train tickets and shunting trains the rest of my life. Fortunately, even before I got the results of the interview, there were new developments.

In June 1972, after one and a half years at St. Peter's, I got a letter from UNHCR informing me I had been given a place at Dar es Salaam Teachers' College to pursue a Diploma in Education programme, and that UNHCR would offer a full scholarship for my studies. I was overjoyed. Although my dream was to do a degree programme, this was a first step in the right direction.

In July 1972, I said goodbye to my students at St. Peter's Seminary. I did so with a heavy heart because, during the course of one and a half years, I had really come to be fond of them, and they also liked me very much.

## Formal Training at Dar es Salaam Teachers' College

At Dar es Salaam Teachers' College, I took history and English as my teaching subjects, over and above the education courses: educational psychology, teaching methodology, counselling and guidance among others. Again here I met students from all over the country and started making new friends.

Some teachers made a big impression on me at Dar es Salaam Teachers' College. One of them was Mrs. Gertrude Mongela, who taught us history. She was very systematic in her teaching, and always inculcated in us a sense of patriotism and pride in our African identity. With hindsight, it is not surprising that Mrs. Mongela became a respected politician later in her life. Mrs. Kurtz, another history teacher, was from Germany, but had lived in Tanzania for a long time. She was known for being a no nonsense woman and very efficient in whatever she was doing. She was also a very good teacher and helpful to students. I will never forget a comment she made on my teaching practice report. She had been sitting in my history class. I was teaching Form Two West African History. At the end of the lesson, she commented on my report form: "When I learn something from the student I am supervising, I know it has been a good lesson. I have learnt a lot from this lesson." This remark transported me to the skies! I was very happy I had made a good impression on my teacher.

My stay at the Dar es Salaam Teachers' College was rather short. This was a one year programme leading to a Diploma in Education. I was, however, determined to learn as much as I could within that short period of time, since my aim was to make this a stepping stone to higher education. At the end of the programme, I got my Diploma in Education and was posted to teach English at Tabora Girls' Secondary School. I also got a "student of good conduct" prize. To be honest, to this day I don't know the criteria used to identify me for this prize. "Good conduct" is a relative term, so I just assume those who decided to nominate me for the prize had their reasons. It could be that I got this prize because I am a rather quiet person. If so, it is interesting that my teachers saw this as a positive attribute, while earlier on at Zaza, the *Frères de la Charité* had seen this characteristic in a negative way. I had been, on several occasions, warned not to be "too quiet." It could be the case that at Zaza my being "too quiet" was interpreted as being arrogant and disrespectful; or maybe this was an indication that I was a dangerous Tutsi, a snake just quietly waiting to inject its venom in the next unsuspecting victim. This was the unenviable stereotype of the Tutsi at this time. Whatever the case, I think this is an indication that a person's character can be interpreted differently by different people.

In July 1973, just as I was preparing to go to Tabora Girls' Secondary School to take up my new appointment as a teacher, Major-General

Juvénal Habyarimana toppled President Grégoire Kayibanda in a coup d'état in Rwanda. The justification for this *coup d'état*, as explained by the new ruler of Rwanda, was that President Kayibanda had become a dictator and had divided the Rwandese people into ethnic and regional factions. He was especially accused of killing many Tutsis even though they were his in-laws (Kayibanda's wife was a Tutsi). He was also accused of favouring people from his own region, the *abanyanduga* from Gitarama, at the expense of those from other regions. At first many people, including Rwandese in exile, thought Major-General Habyarimana genuinely wanted to heal the wounds and start afresh on a road to peace and reconciliation. However, after the honeymoon, he started showing his true colours. First, it is believed he ordered that the deposed president be starved to death in his house, where he had been put under house arrest. Apparently, the new president was so superstitious that he feared to spill the blood of the person he had deposed, hence the decision to starve him instead. It is said that Grégoire Kayibanda and his wife spent their last painful days eating paper from books in their library and pieces of foam from sofa cushions (Kinzer 2008). As years went by, Major-General Habyarimana did all the things he had accused his predecessor of, and more. He favoured people from his region, he persecuted the Tutsi and even declared there was no room in Rwanda for Tutsis in exile. His rule became very autocratic and all the powers were concentrated in his hands and those of a few trusted relatives, including his wife and her brothers. This clique of people who ran Rwanda was nicknamed *akazu* (literally, a small house). Their word became law.

As Rwandans in exile, we followed these developments in Rwanda with a lot of interest. At the beginning of the Habyarimana regime, we had some hopes that we may at some point in time be able to go back to Rwanda. It became clear later that he had no intention of allowing us back into the country. There were two alternatives for Rwandans in exile: remain in the countries they had taken refuge, or start organising to claim their right to go back to Rwanda. The late 1970s and early 1980s marked the beginning of the advocacy of Rwandans in exile to go back to Rwanda as a right.

## A Career Begins at Tabora Girls' Secondary School

I reported to Tabora Girls' Secondary School in August 1973, at the age of almost 27, to start a career as a teacher. On my arrival, I reported at the house of the Second Master, Mr. Buluda, because it was in the evening and offices were closed. He and his family put me up for the night. The following morning, I was introduced to the Headmistress, Ms. Grace Massawe, and later I was shown a one bedroom flat on the school campus where I would stay. I did not have much luggage, just a suitcase containing my clothes and a few other personal belongings. That day I had to go to town to do some shopping: utensils and crockery as well as some food. I had to start organizing my life as a bachelor teacher. My experiences at St. Peter's came in handy. At least I had learnt how to cook for myself, so this would not be much of a problem.

At that time, both Tabora Girls' and neighbouring Tabora Boys' were 'military' schools. These were supposed to be elite schools where future leaders were to be groomed. For this reason, each of these schools had some military officers assigned to them to inculcate the students with military discipline. Both staff and students had para-military uniforms (khaki trousers, jackets and a cap), which they were expected to wear on special occasions. However, apart from these superficial tokens of some kind of military presence, both schools were ordinary secondary schools like any other in the country.

One of the officers, Captain Chacha (not his real name), always harassed me by reminding me I was a refugee and saying I should go back to my country because I was taking a job that should be given to a Tanzanian. His words were like rubbing salt into a fresh wound; I would really be very sad on such occasions. I would, however, tell him the government knew I was a refugee when I was posted to the school. I had nothing to hide and nothing to apologize for. If he did not like me, it was his problem. I must say such resentment has been expressed by a number of other people both to me and to members of my family, even long after we had acquired Tanzanian citizenship. The tone differs from person to person. Some are outright crude and rude in their comments; others are more subtle in their insinuations. However, the effect is always the same: you feel you are not wanted, despite efforts to contribute to a country you genuinely call your home. At times I wonder whether citizenship by naturalization is really second class citizenship.

I was assigned to teach English in Forms Three and Four. Fortunately, I already had some teaching experience acquired at St. Peter's Seminary, so facing students was not intimidating, even as a young man who had just completed my training. Of course the difference between St. Peter's and Tabora Girls' was that while at the former I was teaching boys, at the latter I was teaching girls. At a relatively young age (I was not much older than some of the Form Five and Six girls), being a male teacher in a girls' school was a bit of a challenge. However, I weathered that storm and for the six years I was at Tabora Girls', I never was involved in any scandal with my students. I learnt later that my nickname was HB (handsome boy). At the time, all I knew was that my students were very eager to learn, so I was motivated to work hard so as not to disappoint them.

Education for Self-Reliance was "practiced" at school in the sense that the school had a farm where students worked after class. Teachers also had plots of land where they could grow maize and vegetables. Usually students volunteered to help teachers work on their plots. Still, farm work was seen by both teachers and students as an appendage to the real responsibility of the school – academic lessons. Mwalimu Nyerere's concept of integrating academic lessons with practical work had not yet taken root.

Apart from teaching, I was also given the responsibility of being in charge of the school library. This role entailed supervising the librarian as well as students who were assigned to assist him on a rotational basis.

When I had stayed for one year at the school, there was one incident concerning the library that disturbed me. One day, the Second Master, Mr. Dimoso (Mr. Buluda had since left the school), went to the library and found students reading when they were supposed to be working outside. He chased them out of the library, ordered the librarian to lock the library and took the keys from him. Later on the librarian told me what had happened. I waited for the Second Master to tell me why he had decided to close the library without informing me, but for two days the library remained closed and I was told nothing. I decided to confront the Second Master. He was very rude to me and said I had no right to question his decisions. I was angry and immediately wrote a letter to the Headmistress to resign my responsibility for the library. When the Headmistress saw the letter, she called me to her office. I told her what had happened. She dissuaded me from resigning and called the Second Master to give his side of the story. In the end the Second Master admitted that he had wronged me and apologized. I accepted the apology and withdrew the resignation letter.

At Tabora Girls' I was also the Secretary of the Disciplinary Committee. One difficult case that is still vivid in my mind is when one male teacher, Mr. Maganga (not his real name) was accused of sexually harassing students. The Disciplinary Committee sat for a whole day and a greater part of the night hearing evidence against the teacher as well as his defence. In the end, there was ample evidence that the teacher was guilty of having sexual relations with several girls, as well as sexually harassing others. The case was reported to the Ministry of Education, and the teacher was dismissed.

Another incident I remember very well at Tabora Girls' is when one day I punished some girls by making them frog march for a couple of minutes. One girl collapsed and was taken to the dispensary. The other girls saw this as an opportunity to get at me. Several of them feigned collapsing, like their fellow student. They were all taken to the dispensary. I immediately stopped the punishment. Fortunately, nothing serious happened to any of them, but this was a lesson for me: no more frog marching of students!

Much as I was happy with my job as a secondary school teacher, I still had a dream of going for further studies. Even though I could now be admitted at the University of Dar es Salaam on account of having a Diploma in Education as "equivalent qualification", I did not have a scholarship. I therefore continued to write to several bodies known to support refugee students, with no success. While waiting for that chance to get a scholarship, I also decided to re-sit my Form Six examinations. I enrolled as a private candidate to re-sit literature. I also was determined to revive my French which I had learnt and used as a medium of instruction at primary school in Rwanda. I therefore took private lessons in French with the aim of doing 'A' level French alongside literature. In 1978 I sat for these two subjects and got 'A' grade in both. With these qualifications, the only obstacle between me and a university education was now my refugee status and lack of a scholarship.

## A Family of My Own

I married Monica Umulikanwa in April 1976. We had met in Karagwe. Both our parents lived in the same refugee settlement, Nkwenda. They were neighbours and good friends. So when I asked for her hand in marriage, there was no resistance at all from her family because they knew me and my family. Unlike my parents, who came from Gisaka in eastern Rwanda, Monica's parents came from Nyanza, Central Rwanda. When they first came to Nkwenda settlement from Burundi where they had taken refuge, they had been warned by friends that most refugees in that settlement were from Gisaka and therefore likely to be witches! As they settled down, they found no evidence of this. Even today, my wife and I sometimes tease each other about our origins in Rwanda, me coming from a region of 'witches' and her coming from a region of 'troublesome and quarrelsome' people.

To cover our wedding expenses, I had to borrow 2000 shillings from a Dutch priest friend of mine, Father Marcel, who was the Director of the Students' Centre in Tabora. To put this into perspective, this amount was more than twice my monthly salary. I agreed with Father Marcel that I would pay him back in small instalments. I did my best to repay the debt, but Father Marcel knew that I was really struggling, so he decided to write off the debt before I had finished repaying it. I was very grateful to him for that gesture.

Our wedding was a very simple ceremony at a makeshift 'church' within the school compound, officiated by Father Marcel and Father Felician Nkwera. At that time, Father Nkwera was still in the mainstream Catholic Church and had not yet started his *Wana Maombi* congregation. The new headmistress, Ms. Cecilia Matemu, hosted a party for us at her residence in the evening, at which all members of staff were invited. Everybody ate, drank to their satisfaction and danced the night away, but at the end of the day, the expenses were minimal because everybody contributed in kind whatever they had in terms of food and drinks. This was really a communal celebration, very different from present day weddings which have become commercialized.

On 15th January 1977, we had a baby boy, baptized Emmanuel. A baby daughter followed almost immediately on 22nd March 1978. She was christened Peace. Because both Emmanuel and Peace were born when both my wife and I were still refugees, they were not Tanzanian citizens, even though they were born in Tanzania. Later when we became citizens by naturalisation, they could renounce their Rwandan citizenship after attaining the age of 18 and become Tanzanian citizens. This is what they did. Life with a young family was not easy. Apart from the salary not being sufficient, our two children were born close to the time of Tanzania's war with the dictator, Idi Amin Dada of Uganda (1978 to 1979). This was the beginning of a long period of economic hardship in Tanzania. My wife and I tried to supplement the meagre salary I got by growing vegetables and maize on the plot of land mentioned above. So at least we were assured of enough food.

While we lived in Tabora, my parents and my wife's parents lived with other refugee families in the Nkwenda refugee settlement in Karagwe. In the 1970s, there was talk that all refugees from Rwanda would be granted Tanzanian citizenship if they wanted. Mwalimu Nyerere said it was absurd for Africans to be refugees on their own continent, just because of arbitrary boundaries drawn by colonialists in Berlin. He called us, refugees in Tanzania, *wahamiaji wakazi* (resident immigrants) rather than *wakimbizi* (refugees). Now, as years went by and Rwanda became more and more of a distant dream, I decided that I would take Tanzanian citizenship if offered that chance. This was in fact the intention of most people living in refugee camps in Karagwe, including our parents.

My efforts to secure a scholarship eventually bore fruit. I secured a full scholarship from UNHCR to study at the University of Dar es Salaam. I got admission for the 1978/79 academic year. Unfortunately, I got the information of my admission rather late. I had to make arrangements to take my family to Karagwe because I could not leave them in Tabora. In Karagwe, they would live near our parents. The alternative of taking them to Dar es Salaam was considered, but it was not feasible mainly because of accommodation difficulties. These arrangements would definitely take time and there was no way I could make it on time to start the new academic year. I therefore asked if UNHCR could guarantee my scholarship for the following academic year; they said they would. I therefore started the process of re-applying for admission for the academic year 1979/80, while at the same time making arrangements to move my family to Karagwe. I also had to ask for release from the Ministry of Education in order to be able to go for further studies.

## Undergraduate Studies at the University of Dar es Salaam

In July 1979, I left my family in Karagwe and went to start my university studies at the University of Dar es Salaam, at the age of 33. We had managed to buy a small plot of land with a banana grove and a simple grass thatched house. The arrangement was that my wife would work on the plot of land to grow food, while I would support her financially with part of my scholarship money. Before I left, I made sure I completed forms to apply for Tanzanian citizenship. These forms were now available in the settlements in Karagwe and elsewhere in Tanzania where Rwandese refugees were living.

At the University of Dar es Salaam, I registered for B.A. (Education), taking Linguistics, French and Literature, as well as Education courses. The UNHCR scholarship covered tuition, meals, accommodation, books and stationery, all paid directly to the university. I was also paid a stipend for other expenses. This stipend was enough to cater for my needs, as well as support my family back in Karagwe. Financially I was, in fact, much better off than when I was teaching at Tabora Girls' Secondary School.

My three years as an undergraduate at the University of Dar es Salaam were very challenging, but also very enjoyable. The challenge was to be away from my family. Fortunately, I could go to visit them at the end of each term. In those days, university students could get concession tickets from Air Tanzania. I therefore used to travel by air to Bukoba, and from there to Karagwe by bus. This way, I could see my family three times a year.

I enjoyed the courses I was taking. Development Studies, which was compulsory for every undergraduate, was especially an eye opener. Theories of development and the relationship between developed and developing countries gave me new insights on the meaning of poverty and mental slavery within the context of power relations between the West and Third World countries. I found Walter Rodney's *How Europe Underdeveloped Africa* and Frantz Fanon's *The Wretched of the Earth* very illuminating.

Looking back, I think people in Tanzania in particular and Africa in general have for a long time taken colonialism as an excuse for making little progress. After fifty years of independence, do we still have any justification for blaming all our ills on colonialism? Instead of singing the song of how Europe underdeveloped Africa, we should be talking about how Africa is under-developing itself. What is the difference between the treaties signed between Carl Peters of Germany and our illiterate forefathers, and the current contracts signed between our educated leaders and the "investors"? At least we can excuse those Africans who dealt with the likes of Carl Peters for their ignorance. Nyerere once said, in order to develop, we need four things: people, land, good policies and good leadership. By people, he probably meant a human resource which is well educated. You can have people, but if they don't have the requisite knowledge and skills, especially in the current knowledge-based society, it is very difficult to get development. In many African countries today, the majority of the people are not well educated. In this 21$^{st}$ century, we have people who still believe you can get rich by killing an albino and selling his/her body parts. Land (and by extension other natural resources) is important, but there are countries with very little land and very few natural resources which are developed. Switzerland and Singapore are two good examples. Conversely, Africa with its vast natural resources is still poor. Nigeria is an important producer of oil, yet fuel shortages are endemic in that country. The Democratic Republic of the Congo is one of the richest countries in mineral deposits, yet it is one of the poorest in the world in terms of economic development. Good policies and good leadership are, in my view, in short supply in many African countries. So, of the four ingredients of development identified by Nyerere, Africa has one in abundance (land and natural resources), but falls short in the three others. I think this is what is holding us back, not the colonial legacy as our rulers would like us to believe.

Dr. Jennifer Higham, Dr. Christopher Elderkin and Prof. Herman Batibo introduced me to the mysteries of linguistics. I really enjoyed their lectures. Of my French lecturers, I especially have fond memories of the late Dr. Abel Magoti. We all, his students, liked him because he was so knowledgeable and committed to his work. He was also very strict, but fair. He was, by any standards, an excellent lecturer. Prof. Abel Ishumi was one of my favourite lecturers in Education. In literature, lectures by Prof. Gabriel Ruhumbika and the late Dr. Grant Kamenju were very enjoyable. Dr. Kamenju was well known for his revolutionary, anti-colonial stance. Unfortunately, he later became an alcoholic. He returned to Kenya, his home country and died there.

At the end of my first year, I was given the Vice Chancellor's award for first year best student in the Faculty of Arts and Social Sciences. It was Tshs. 500 cash, quite a substantial amount in those days!

On 5th December 1980, just four days before my 34th birthday, my certificate of naturalization as a Tanzanian citizen was signed in Dar es Salaam. I was in my second year. This was a big day for me because now I had a country I could call my home. From 1962 to 1980 I had been stateless. The UNHCR agreed to maintain the scholarship until I completed my undergraduate studies.

At the end of the second year, the French class had a study tour for three months at the University of Burundi. This tour was meant to give us some opportunity to practice our French in a Francophone country. In previous years, students of French had been going to the university in Besançon in France. This time the French Embassy in Dar es Salaam said sending students to France was very expensive, so they decided to sponsor our trip to Burundi instead. Our class had two groups of students: the Education students, of which I was one, and International Relations students. We were sent to Burundi because it is supposed to be a 'Francophone' country. However, apart from the French we were taught in class, the environment in Bujumbura was anything but 'Francophone'. Most people we interacted with spoke either Kirundi or Kiswahili. Very few spoke French. As a Kinyarwanda speaker, I could very easily speak my language and understand Kirundi speakers without any problem. The two languages are so similar that they could in fact be called dialects of the same language. I also had friends and relatives who lived in Bujumbura, so for me it was some kind of homecoming. For this reason, I don't think the environment was very conducive for learning French.

Not all was positive or educational at the premier university of Tanzania. One activity engaged in by students at the University of Dar es Salaam which is still vivid in my mind was the wall literature, or the so-called *Mzee Punch*. Students would put up stories that scandalized other students, especially female students. These stories were put up on the cafeteria walls, very high up, where they would not be easy to remove. The stories were put up at night, and it was very difficult to identify the people who did this as they did not sign their names. This wall literature was ostensibly meant to 'discipline' students and prevent them from engaging in anti-social behaviour. However, the bulk of the literature was directed at female students, and it was often used to settle personal scores. If a male student was refused sexual favours by a female student, the former would use Mzee Punch to scandalize the latter. The so-called 'revelations' about the female student would, in most cases, be untrue, but many people would believe them anyway. For many female students this was a catch 22 situation: if they agreed to sexual advances, they would be exposed for being 'prostitutes'; if they refused, they would still be exposed. They would be accused of being frigid or *frumo* (frustrated mothers), or past scandals, whether true or false, would be revealed about them. This wall was nothing less than sexual harassment. Many female students had to live with this kind of harassment and the university administration seemed not to care about it.

This state of affairs continued for the whole time I was an undergraduate student and well after I had graduated. In 1991, when I was already a member of staff at the University of Dar es Salaam, a tragic incident shook the university. A student by the name of Levina Mukasa committed suicide because of sexual harassment associated with the wall literature. It had to go to this extent for the university to wake up from its stupor. The wall literature was banned immediately. Unfortunately, it took the life of an innocent woman for the university and the nation to act.

1982 was a year of upheavals and transition for both me and my family. When I completed my undergraduate studies in March 1982, I was assigned by the Ministry of Education to go to Milambo Secondary School in Tabora to teach French. However, the Department of Foreign Languages and Linguistics had also offered me a position as a Tutorial

Assistant. I had wanted to be in the French section of the Department, but I was told by the Head of Department, Dr. Batibo, that there was no vacancy at that time. I was, instead, offered a place in the recently established Communication Skills Unit by the Coordinator of the Unit, Dr. Pauline Rea. I wanted to remain at the university as a Tutorial Assistant, but for this to happen I had to get clearance from the Ministry of Education. This proved a bit tricky. The Ministry insisted I had to report to my work station and apply for clearance from there.

The University administration tried to get me cleared before going to Tabora. I especially recognize the efforts made by Prof. Geofrey Mmari, Chief Academic Officer at that time, and Mr. Edward Jambo, Senior Administrative Officer, on my behalf. I had the impression that the Head of Department was actually not very enthusiastic about my joining the department, that he could have accepted me in the French section. While the individuals mentioned above were trying to get me released by the government, the Head of Department was the one insisting that I had to go to Tabora first.

Despite all these efforts, the Ministry insisted I had to report to Milambo. So, I went to Karagwe, took my family and reported to Milambo. Meanwhile, efforts to get my release from the Ministry continued at the University of Dar es Salaam. In July 1982, I was released by the Ministry and reported to the University. I had not even started teaching at Milambo Secondary School, but the Ministry of Education had spent money to relocate my family from Karagwe to Tabora. Bureaucratic red tape can be absurd.

At Milambo Secondary School, my family and I had been invited by a friend who was also a teacher at the school, Mr. Rutagengwa, to stay with him while we were looking for a house as there was no available house at the school. Mr. Rutagengwa had been my 'best man' during my marriage ceremony when I was at Tabora Girls' Secondary School. We stayed in his house for about a week, and then we got a small mud walled room (no electricity, no running water, no hard floor) to rent near the school. The room was so small that we had to keep the utensils under the bed. Let me remind the reader that at this time we already had two children and my wife was expecting a third child. So this was a really difficult situation, and for the sake of my pregnant wife and our small children, I already knew that, whatever happened, we could not afford to stay there for a long time.

On getting word of my release by the Ministry of Education, I left my family in the small rented room in Tabora and went to Dar es Salaam.

The University could not offer me a house, but I had the option of staying in a hotel with my family until housing became available on campus. I decided to take that option. I was given two hotel rooms at the Africana Hotel. My family joined me from Tabora. The arrangement was full board covered by the University, but staff staying at the hotel had to contribute a percentage of their salary to cover some of the expenses. The University provided transport to and from campus, and staff could take a lunch box from the hotel if they wished. I stayed at the Africana Hotel with my family from July to September, 1982.

This was a new chapter in my life. I was now leaving behind the career of a secondary school teacher and embarking on a career of a University lecturer. I was excited because of the opportunity of advancing myself educationally and being able to contribute to the education of others, but I was also apprehensive at the same time, not knowing what this new chapter had in store for me.

## Academic Initiation at Lancaster University

The Department of Foreign Languages and Linguistics, through the effort of Dr. Pauline Rea, had secured a British Council scholarship for me to go for M.A. studies at Lancaster University in the UK. If there is anybody to whom I owe my initiation into the academic world, it is Pauline Rea. Without her inviting me as a Tutorial Assistant in the Communication Skills Unit, I would have gone to teach French at Milambo Secondary School and my life would have taken a different turn.

I was to leave for the UK in September 1982. The problem was that my wife was expecting our third baby. We were in a dilemma. If I declined this scholarship, there was no guarantee that I would get another one. If I went, who would take care of my family, especially with a new baby on the way? This was one of the most difficult decisions that I had to make in my whole life. In the end my wife and I decided that I should go. My flight was booked for 25th September 1982. On that day, the baby was born in the morning; my flight was in the evening. I was able to see the baby and spend a few hours with him. We called him Safari for obvious reasons. In Kiswahili, the word means journey, so he was born on the day his father left for a journey that would keep him away from home for a whole year.

That evening, I left my family in our one room at the so called Research Flats on the University of Dar es Salaam Mlimani campus. I boarded a British Airways flight to London Heathrow via Nairobi. The flight to London was long and tiring. This was my first journey overseas, so I had mixed feelings. On the one hand, I had just left my family alone and I was going to a new country not knowing what I would find there. On the other hand, there was a feeling of excitement, of going to discover a different world altogether. Didn't Europeans 'discover' Africa just because they were seeing it for the first time? In this sense, this was going to be my personal discovery of Europe.

We touched down at Heathrow in the early hours of 26th September 1982. I had prepared myself for the cold weather. After the immigration clearance, I got my luggage and proceeded to the underground station. I had been given clear instructions at the British Council in Dar es Salaam. I was to go to Victoria Station where a British Council courier would meet me, and this is exactly what happened. At Victoria Station, I was given some money and a train ticket to Lancaster. I went into the underground again and headed for Euston Station, where I boarded the train to Lancaster. My first culture shock, both in the underground train in London and on the Lancaster-bound train, was to realize that unlike in Africa, passengers didn't talk to each other. Everyone was reading either a newspaper or a book. You don't talk even to the person seated next to you. If you were lucky, you got a feigned smile; I wondered if this behaviour was the proverbial English stiff upper lip.

Everything was so fast, so efficient and so precise. In three hours I was at Lancaster. There was no time for anything to sink in my brain, apart from the fact that for the first time in my life, I realized that I was black. When you are surrounded by black people like you, you take your skin colour for granted; you are not conscious of it. When I arrived in England, I, for the first time, realized that my skin colour was different. I was a little bit scared.

The same precision and efficiency I had experienced in London manifested itself in Lancaster. From the railway station, I took a taxi to the university. I had been told where to report on arrival: the Porter's Lodge at Bowland College. On arrival at the Porter's Lodge, I was given the keys to my room and a dossier introducing me to the university. The room was already made, clean sheets, and everything was in place. It was like checking in at a hotel. It was very different from my shared room at the University of Dar es Salaam as an undergraduate student. Here I had a room of my own, with shared bathroom facilities for four people on the same corridor. There were also kitchen facilities, so students could prepare their own meals if they so wished, or they could eat in the different cafeterias on campus.

The following day, I reported at the Department of Linguistics and Modern English Language, also in Bowland College. I was registered in the M.A. (English Language Teaching) programme. The majority of students in this programme were from the United Kingdom, but there were also students from different parts of the world. I was the only black African in the programme, but there was a white South African woman in my class. In those days, and especially for somebody from Tanzania, trying to relate to a white South African was a big challenge. However, we were both polite to each other. In any case, she said she did not like apartheid. This might have been sincere or it might have been said in order to please me. Whatever the case, I gave her the benefit of doubt. There were also, as far as I can remember, students from India, South Korea, Mexico, Jordan, Hong Kong and Syria. In the same department but in a different programme (M.A. Language Studies) there was another African, from Senegal. His name was Babakar Ndiaye. We became very good friends. Unfortunately we have lost contact.

Lancaster University campus is very beautiful. It is pitched on a hill some five kilometres from Lancaster city centre. When I arrived, it was the beginning of autumn, so tree leaves were starting to change into golden colours; it was a wonderful sight. The lawns were very well kept and all the buildings were well maintained. Later on, when winter came, I was fascinated by snow, which I was seeing for the first time in my life. Winter was not as bad as I had feared. The temperature never fell below zero degrees Celsius. I was also well prepared in terms of having the right clothes. Indoors, all the buildings were connected to the central heating system. It was a bit difficult to get used to the short days and long nights in winter, just as it was to experience long days and short nights in summer.

The M.A. (ELT) programme was very intensive. We had to complete everything in 12 months, both course-work and the dissertation. We therefore had to work very hard. At Lancaster, I came to realize that English language teaching is big business both in the UK and the USA. As mentioned above, the majority of students on the M.A. (ELT) programme were British. Most of them had been English language experts in different parts of the world. They now wanted to get more qualifications in order to be able to compete on the ELT market world-wide. Indeed, later on one of my classmates came to Tanzania as an English language expert under the auspices of the British government funded English Language Teaching Support Project (ELTSP). Although we had the same qualifications and he was not necessarily brighter than me, he now qualified to be an expert in teaching English in Tanzania while I, with the advantage of local knowledge and experience of teaching English in the country, did not qualify. The only difference between him and me was that he was British and the ELTSP was a British-funded project. I also realized that teaching English was not just a technical job of imparting knowledge and language skills to learners. It was also a socio-economic/political project of the distribution of cultural resources. Who gets access to English and who doesn't? Who benefits from the ELT business? These questions kept lingering in my mind and later they shaped my thinking about my role as a teacher of English in a Third World country.

We had some of the best lecturers in the field of linguistics – well respected academics not only in the UK, but also world-wide: Prof. Geoffrey Leech (grammar and semantics), Prof. Christopher Candlin (second language teaching and discourse), Dr. Norman Fairclough (discourse), Dr. Marilyn Martin-Jones (bilingualism), Dr. Francis Katamba (phonology and morphology), Dr. Richard Allright (second language teaching) to mention a few.

Francis Katamba, a Ugandan married to a Scottish woman, was not only my lecturer, he was also a very welcoming person who made all African students at Lancaster feel at home in his house. He and his wife, Janet, would, whenever they could, invite us to their home for dinner. In a relatively small city like Lancaster, racially mixed families were not very common. In fact, Dr. Katamba's wife was always teased by her colleagues at the school where she was teaching as being the Scottish woman with an African name, who teaches French.

The other person in the department I became close to was Marilyn Martin-Jones. I joined her Bilingualism Research Group. Her interest in bilingualism partly stemmed from the fact that she was Welsh, and bilingual in Welsh and English. From the discussions we had in this group, I started developing interest in language in education issues, especially in multilingual societies. It was during these discussions that my ideas on the role of language in education sharpened. I was later (1990-1992) to work with Marilyn Martin-Jones as my Ph.D. supervisor. She is, no doubt, my intellectual mentor.

Although I never experienced overt racism at Lancaster during my first year at the university, there were conversations with white people that had racist undertones. Once, a student with whom I shared the kitchen said that nothing spectacular had ever come from Africa. It was clear to me that his view of Africa was from the distorted history of the continent written by misguided white people. I challenged him to read about the ancient kingdoms of Ghana, Songhay and Mali in West Africa and Great Zimbabwe in southern Africa. I told him to read the works of Basil Davidson, Walter Rodney and Cheikh Anta Diop. From these he would see that Africa is not and has never been a 'dark continent'. He was surprised to hear that Timbuktu was a great centre of learning as far back as the 13th century, and that Ethiopians were literate when Europe was still in the dark ages. I told him that European explorers never discovered Africa; they were just the first Europeans to see it.

Sometimes during conversations with British people, I would be told that the British are not racist, but that there was institutional racism. I failed to understand how an institution could be racist. If there was institutional racism, surely it was because at least some of the people working in those institutions were racist. At other times I would get irritating questions, which again had racist undertones. I would be asked, for example, whether in Africa people live with animals in the national parks, or how I had come to Europe when in Africa there were no airplanes. Some of the questions and comments smacked of racism; others were outright ignorant. Once I told somebody that I was from Tanzania, and he asked whether Tanzania was in Nairobi! I know of only one state which is inside a city, the Vatican in Rome.

I experienced an incident of overt racism when I went back to Lancaster for my Ph.D. studies. During my final year, I had to look for off campus accommodation. The Student Union usually advertised accommodation which was available off campus, and students who were in need would follow up these leads and make private arrangements with landlords/landladies. One day I phoned one such place that had just been advertised and the person on the other end of the line said the room had already been taken. I suspected she had declined to give me the room because of my African accent. I wanted to check if what I suspected was true. I asked a British student to phone the landlady making the same inquiry, and he was told the room was available. My suspicion was confirmed; I was denied the room because I was an African. I did not bother to go physically because I knew I would not get the room. I eventually got a room in a house that belonged to a fellow Ph.D. student.

During the year I was at Lancaster, I could only correspond with my wife back in Dar es Salaam. Life was very difficult in Tanzania because of economic hardships. From a distance, I was able to support my family rom my scholarship money. I sent some money to Pauline Rea, who was still at the University of Dar es Salaam, who would then pass it on to my wife.

To give a sense of the kind of economic difficulties in Tanzania at that time is difficult. There was virtually nothing in the shops. If one wanted to buy a kilo of sugar, one had to know people who sold this sugar (or any other goods) at a price way above the government recommended price. Because this was illegal, people who sold these everyday necessities of life would only agree to sell to you if they trusted you would not report them to the authorities. People had to learn how to survive by establishing networks of who knows who has something to sell. During these difficult times, the joke went around that when you see people queuing, don't ask what is on offer; just join the queue because you will need whatever is being sold. This is indeed what many people did. The University of Dar es Salaam tried to help staff members by buying foodstuffs from the Regional Trading Corporation (RTC) in order to sell these to staff at official retail prices. However, because of the acute shortages, sometimes people were forced to buy even food not fit for human consumption. For example, if you wanted to buy a kilo of sugar or wheat flour, you could do that on condition that you also buy a kilo of virtually rotten cassava flour which you just threw away. These difficult economic times lasted from 1979 to 1985.

In September 1983, I completed my M.A. studies and went back to Tanzania. In those days, if you got a chance to go abroad you would be expected to bring all sorts of things that were not available in Tanzania: toilet soap, toothpaste, clothes, etc. But how much could one carry, even if one had all the money in the world? At that time, even people with money were restricted in what they could buy. For example, people who had stayed overseas and had saved some money could not buy a car and ship it to Tanzania. Only pick-ups were allowed, and for this one had to get permission from the government. Foreign exchange was so controlled that if one wanted to travel abroad; one had to get clearance from the President's office in order to be able to purchase foreign currency.

I bought whatever I could, packed and flew back home. Apart from the mundane items that would otherwise be taken for granted and which I would not have bought had Tanzania been in a better economic position, the only thing of value that I bought was an electric sewing machine for my wife. I shipped it before leaving Lancaster.

I came back from England, having successfully completed my M.A. for English Language Teaching, with 'the tools of trade' that would help me to do my job as a university lecturer more effectively. I had consolidated not only my knowledge of second/foreign language teaching, but also my proficiency in the English language. Having stayed in England for a whole year in an English speaking environment certainly helped me improve my English language skills. This was a real Anglophone country. It was worlds apart from my 'francophone' experience in Burundi! I came back with confidence that I would be able to put to good use the knowledge obtained at Lancaster.

Chapter Four

# The University of Dar es Salaam

## A Refugee's Difficult Dilemma

When I arrived in Dar es Salaam, my wife and our three children were still living in the one room flat on campus. Safari was now one year old. The other children, Emmanuel and Peace, were also, needless to say, bigger than when I left them. I was relieved that the whole family was safe and healthy, despite all the hardships. My wife must have really found it very difficult, but in the end she made it. I was thankful for her courage and perseverance. My priority was now to get a bigger house. Towards the end of 1983, we were allocated a three bedroom house on campus.

Immediately on return, now as an Assistant Lecturer, I was assigned to teach Communication Skills to first year students in the Faculty of Law. Not being a lawyer, I found this rather challenging. I had come back with theories of English language teaching, but legal communication was specialized. I therefore had to start reading law books, especially those on legal method, in order to be able to teach effectively. I enjoyed reading these books and I found them very useful. I could now apply my language teaching theories to practical communication in the field of law. In fact, my students thought I was a lawyer until I told them I wasn't!

Having completed my M.A., my next step was now to go for Ph.D. studies. Getting admission at Lancaster University would not be a problem. They already knew me and my performance in M.A. studies had been good. I therefore had the qualifications to enrol in the Ph.D. programme; the problem was how to get a scholarship. However, even if I got a scholarship, going back to Europe immediately was out of the question for two main reasons. First, I had been away from my family for a long time. Leaving again so soon would not be fair to them. In fact, my wife told me that our daughter, Peace, had complained at a very young age of four that she did not understand why every time I take them to a place, I leave them there alone and go away. I had left them in Karagwe for three years in order to go for my undergraduate studies. I left them for a short period of time in Tabora, while making arrangements to be employed by the University of Dar es Salaam. I left them again for one year in order to go for further studies in England. I think my daughter had a point! I therefore needed to be with them at least for a couple of years before I thought of travelling again. Second, the University would not let me go for further studies immediately. There was a shortage of academic staff in the Communication Skills Unit, so I had to work for some time before approval to go for further studies would be considered.

When we resettled in a bigger house, the situation was much better for children. Our children could now play with neighbourhood children, and they were less constrained in terms of space. At the Research Flats, they had been really penned in with very little room for manoeuvre. This move also coincided with the time when our first born, Emmanuel, started school at the nearest primary school, which was fortunately only about two hundred metres from our new home.

Sadly, both at school and at the playground near our house, our children were sometimes harassed by other children, telling them that they were not Tanzanians and that they should go back home. There is no way these children were saying this on their own; they must have heard such comments from their parents. This made us very sad. Why were we not accepted even after acquiring Tanzanian citizenship? How would we explain this situation to our children, who only knew Tanzania? The only thing we could tell them was to ignore the children who were tormenting them. However, it reached a point where the children of one particular family were harassing our children so much that my wife faced this family and told them point blank that they should stop this kind of nonsense. That did the trick. From that time onwards, the harassment was substantially reduced to just occasional innuendoes about people from a "neighbouring country" who have come to take jobs from Tanzanians.

Meanwhile, Rwandan people in exile were still talking about the possibility of going back home. Given the phobia against refugees and the desire to have a place to belong, this desire was very understandable. In a way refugees in Tanzania were more fortunate than those in the other countries in the region. This was because of Nyerere's stance on how refugees should be treated. He believed in integrating refugees from African countries into the Tanzanian community and eventually granting them citizenship. The situation in Uganda, Kenya and Zaire (DR Congo) was different. In these countries refugees from Rwanda were not treated well. This was especially so in Uganda during President Obote's second administration in the early 1980s. However, the Habyarimana regime in Rwanda had made it clear that Rwandese refugees were not welcome back into Rwanda. His argument was that the country was very small, so it would not accommodate everybody. In other words, he was, in fact, saying that he did not recognize Rwandese people in exile as *bona fide* citizens of Rwanda. That obviously was not acceptable to many people who wanted to return to their country. In 1979, the Rwandese Alliance for National Unity (RANU) was formed by some Rwandese in the diaspora. The objective was to mobilize all Rwandese to start strategizing on how to go back to Rwanda. In 1982, Alexandre Kimenyi, a professor of linguistics of Rwandese origin at California State University, Sacramento, launched a magazine called *Impuruza* (the herald) in the USA. The aim was to rally all Rwandese in the diaspora to start talking openly about going back home. The government in Rwanda was not amused. Everything was done, by hook or by crook, to derail these initiatives. They were not successful. Instead, the circulation of the magazine and the discussions started by RANU spread to all corners of the world where there were Rwandese in exile. In 1987, RANU transformed itself into the Rwandese Patriotic Front (RPF) whose objectives were, among other things, to promote national unity and reconciliation, and to repatriate and resettle back into Rwanda all Rwandese refugees in the diaspora.

In Tanzania, as in many other countries in the world where there were Rwandese in exile, people were mobilized through articles in *Impuruza* and through informal discussions during social events. For the first time since the 1959 wave of refugees, there was hope that it was actually possible to go back to Rwanda.

Meanwhile, I continued my academic development and career. Between 1983 and 1989 I continued teaching Communication Skills in the Faculty of Law. In 1987 I was promoted to the rank of Lecturer. I also continued applying for scholarships in different universities. In 1988 through my contact with Prof. Christopher Candlin, who had been my professor at Lancaster University and was now at Macquarie University in Australia, I got a partial scholarship at Macquarie University covering only fees. I needed to secure additional funds to cover my air ticket and living expenses. Unfortunately, the University of Dar es Salaam was not able to support me, so I had to decline this offer. I also kept contacts with the University of Lancaster. Through the Lancaster-Dar es Salaam cooperation agreement, I was able to go to the University of Lancaster three times on short study visits lasting about six weeks each. During these visits I was able to develop my Ph.D. research proposal, under the mentorship of Dr. Marilyn Martin-Jones.

A terrible event happened to my family in June 1988. Our two year old son, Kenneth Rwagaju, our fourth child, suddenly passed away. One afternoon, he was in his bed asleep. Peace, his ten year old sister, went into the room. She came back running and told us that Kenneth was not breathing properly. My wife and I rushed to the room, only to find Kenneth struggling to breathe. We immediately rushed him to the University Health Centre, where he was taken into the consultation room. The doctor told us to wait outside. After a few minutes, he came to us grim faced and simply said, *"bahati mbaya"* (bad luck). We knew Kenneth was already dead. I couldn't hold my tears. When the nurse who had been in the consultation room with the doctor saw me crying, she admonished me and told me to behave like a man.

This was the first death of a close member of the family, and it shocked all of us. Personally, it left me with a lot of unanswered questions. Why should an innocent young child die? What had he done to deserve this? Of course people who came to console us told us it was the will of God, the usual cliché that we loved our son, but God loved him more. As parents of the boy, this was no consolation and it tried our faith in God. If God loved our son more than we did, why did He take him away? Did God show His love by killing the people He loves? Did He not love us as well? No doubt these are questions that anyone who loses a loved one would ask themselves, without any coherent answer.

In October 1989, I got a British Council sandwich scholarship to do my Ph.D. at the University of Lancaster. Under this scholarship, I had to stay at Lancaster for the first year of my study, go back to Tanzania for my second year to collect and analyse data, and return to Lancaster for the final year to write my thesis. This was a convenient arrangement for me, especially given the fact that the scholarship did not cover a family allowance. This meant I could not go with my family. A sandwich programme would therefore allow me to be with my family during the second year of study.

The obvious person at Lancaster to supervise my Ph.D. programme was Dr. Marilyn Martin-Jones because I had worked with her when I was developing my research proposal. Since I had already been to Lancaster several times, settling in was very easy. I knew my way around the campus, and since I had stayed for a whole year before, I knew what to expect in terms of the weather. Also, many of the academic staff members I had left in the Department of Linguistics and Modern English Language in 1983 were still there.

The Ph.D. programme at Lancaster University was by thesis only; there was no coursework component. So, I worked on my own, under the guidance of the supervisor. The Department of Linguistics and Modern English Language had several research groups in which graduate students could meet and exchange ideas on their work. I joined the Bilingualism Research Group and found it very useful. All students working on topics related to bilingualism and language in education were in this group. Because of the diversity of our backgrounds, we really learnt from each other and supported each other in our rather lonely research.

In October 1990, my wife came to visit me at Lancaster. She was with our daughter, Grace, now number four in the line of succession! She was 18 months old at that time, so, although I took them to several places in England, she cannot remember anything of that trip abroad. Her siblings usually tease her that it was a wasted opportunity.

The day my wife arrived, the 1st of October, we heard that RPF fighters had crossed into Rwanda from Uganda. They were under Major-General Fred Rwigema, who had hitherto been a very high ranking military officer in the Ugandan army. The war to force the Government of Major-General Juvénal Habyarimana to accept exiled Rwandese back into their country had begun. However, the events during the first few days of the RPF invasion were not good for the RPF. The leader of the RPF fighters, Fred Rwigema, was killed on the second day of the invasion in mysterious circumstances. One theory is that he was killed in a plot hatched by his two Second-in-Command officers, Major Peter Bayingana and Major Bunyenyezi. The other theory is that he stepped on a land mine, very unlikely on the second day of the conflict. The more likely explanation is that he was shot by a fleeing soldier of the Rwandese army. The death of Major-General Fred Rwigema was a big blow to the RPF. Major Paul Kagame, who was in the USA at the time of invasion, came immediately and took charge of the fighting. France, DR Congo and Belgium immediately came to the assistance of the Habyarimana regime (Prunier,1994).

This invasion was the beginning of a protracted war. Rwandese people in the diaspora were mobilized to contribute to the war effort. Efforts included cash contributions and contributions in kind (e.g. cattle, crops etc. were given to feed the fighters, or they were sold to raise the needed cash). At the same time, young men and women in the diaspora were mobilized to actually go to the battle front and fight for their country. In Tanzania, as elsewhere in the East African region, some students of Rwandese origin abandoned school and went to the war front. Within Rwanda, young Tutsi men and women who felt threatened by the regime joined the RPF, as a way of self-defence because they risked being arrested and imprisoned by the government for being ibyitso (collaborators of the RPF).

The mobilization employed several strategies, one of which was to convince people of Rwandese origin, wherever they were, to take an oath of allegiance to the RPF. I personally never took this oath of allegiance, although I did contribute to the war effort. I did not see any reason why I should take an oath. I supported the effort to allow Rwandese people who wanted to go back to their country to do so, and I contributed in kind to facilitate this effort, albeit in a small way. This for me was enough. I was, in fact, never a card carrying member of the RPF. This non-compliance on my part did not go down well with some RPF cadres in Tanzania, but I did not care what they thought of me, as long as I was convinced I was doing the right thing. This approach has been my stand even with regard to the politics of Tanzania. I have never been a card carrying member of any political party. At election time, I vote for the party of my choice, taking into consideration which party I think will deliver on its promises to the people.

In March 1991, I returned to Tanzania for field work. During this second year of my study, over and above doing field work for my thesis, I continued to teach in the Faculty of Law. In July 1991, I was promoted to the rank of Senior Lecturer. I had, since 1987 when I was promoted to the rank of Lecturer, managed to get enough publications to warrant my promotion to the next level. At that time, a Ph.D. was not a prerequisite for promotion to Senior Lecturer.

In March 1992, I went back to Lancaster for my final year. I had already collected my data and partly analysed it, so I was going to complete data analysis and to write my thesis. I spent the rest of 1992 doing data analysis and writing my thesis under the supervision of Dr. Marilyn Martin-Jones. Between January and March 1993, I was doing final corrections on the thesis, but was also employed on a part-time basis as a tutor in the Department of Linguistics and Modern English Language. I gave lectures on bilingual education in multilingual societies, with a special focus on Africa. I successfully defended my thesis in January 1993.

When congratulating me, Dr. Martin-Jones teased me by saying I deserved two Ph.D.s, one for the research I had done and the other for successfully word-processing the thesis on my own. I had just learnt to use the computer when I was registered for my Ph.D., so word-processing my thesis without any assistance was a great achievement indeed. It is amazing how technology grows very fast. When at Lancaster doing my M.A. degree in the early 1980s, word processing was a distant dream even in Europe, let alone Africa. My M.A. dissertation was typed on the good old fashioned typewriter, with correction fluid to correct any mistake done during the process of typing. In those days, the e-mail service was unheard of. I had to write handwritten letters and send them by airmail if I wanted to communicate with anyone back in Dar es Salaam. It would take two to three weeks for the return mail to reach me. While doing my Ph.D. studies at Lancaster, I was able to produce several publications, including a paper in an international journal and two edited books (Rubagumya 1990, 1991, 1994).The two edited books were a result of research workshops conducted at the University of Dar es Salaam in collaboration with colleagues at Lancaster University. My Ph.D. Supervisor, Dr. Marilyn Martin-Jones, played a big role in the running of these workshops and encouraged me to edit and publish a selection of papers from the workshops. The two volumes were published by Multilingual Matters Ltd., a publishing house based in Clevedon, near Bristol. The Managing Director of the publishing house and his wife, Mike and Marjukka Grover, became very good friends of mine. They had become interested in publishing books on bilingualism for family reasons: Mike is British, while his wife Marjukka is Finnish. To ensure their two sons were bilingual in both English and Finnish, the arrangement in the house was that Mike would always talk to the children in English, while Marjukka would talk to them in Finnish. This worked very well and today the two young men are fluent in both languages.

While at Lancaster, I was invited by several universities in England to give talks and lectures on bilingualism in Tanzania. Among them were Leeds University, Ealing College of Higher Education, the Institute of Education of the University of London, Edge Hill College of Higher Education and the University of York. In all these universities, there were people who knew me personally (especially because of the Lancaster connection) or who had worked in Tanzania and were therefore interested in what was going on in the Tanzanian educational system.

Towards the end of March 1993, I flew back to Tanzania. I was excited because I now had a Ph.D. It was a new status for me, because I would henceforth be addressed as Dr. Rubagumya. However, my ten year old son, Safari, was not impressed. When I showed him my thesis, he could not understand why I had spent three years just writing one 300 page volume! I tried to explain to him that a lot of work needs to be put in; it is not just writing 300 pages. I am sure he still was not impressed even after my explanation. I settled back into my teaching job. With a new qualification, I was now expected to teach both undergraduate and graduate students, as well as supervise M.A. students.

The invasion by the RPF had forced the Habyarimana regime to the negotiating table. Between July 1992 and August 1993, the regime and the RPF were involved in peace talks in Arusha. However, these negotiations were characterized by problems right from the start. Hardliners in Habyarimana's government and in his party, the MRND, did not want to share power with the RPF, so they did everything in their power to sabotage the Arusha talks. This effort included violence within Rwanda to intimidate the Tutsi population as well as the opposition political parties. Hate speeches by Léon Mugesera, a radical member of the MRND, openly encouraged the Hutu to go out and kill their Tutsi neighbours, as the extract below shows:

> "We have to take responsibility in our hands and wipe out these hoodlums[...] The fatal mistake we made in 1959 was to let them (the Tutsi) get out[...] They belong in Ethiopia and we are going to find them a shortcut to get there by throwing them into Nyabarongo River. I must insist on this point. We have to act. Wipe them all out." (Prunier p.172).

On 4th August 1993 a peace agreement was signed in Arusha between the Habyarimana government and the RPF, but it was a very fragile agreement. Neither party was totally satisfied with it, but it was better than no agreement at all. The time between August 1993 and April 1994 was a time of uncertainty in Rwanda. President Habyarimana procrastinated in implementing the Arusha accord. The handing over of power to the transitional government was postponed on several occasions with no convincing reason given. Meanwhile, inside Rwanda the hardliners were arming themselves. They were prepared for a showdown with the President if need be, and they would maintain the status quo at any cost. Pressure by the international community and by the regional leaders increased on President Habyarimana. On 6th April 1994, he was summoned to Dar es Salaam. The presidents of Tanzania, Uganda, Burundi and the vice-president of Kenya were all in the meeting. They told him in no uncertain terms that he had to implement the 1993 Arusha accord. He boarded his plane in the evening of the same day to return to Kigali. He was with President Cyprien Ntaryamira of Burundi on that fateful flight. They never reached their destination.

In the morning of 7th April 1994, I was in my office when my wife came in, breathless, and announced to me that President Habyarimana of Rwanda was dead. His plane had been brought down the previous night when it was approaching Kigali airport from Dar es Salaam. The plane had, by a rather macabre coincidence, actually crashed in his compound in Kigali. Instinctively, I told her the news is not so good because it spelled trouble. This was the beginning of the genocide in Rwanda.

April to July 1994 was hell in Rwanda. It is estimated that about one million people, mainly Tutsi, but also moderate Hutu, were killed in 100 days. The aim of the perpetrators of the genocide was to ensure total extermination of all Tutsi in Rwanda. It was called the "final solution."

One of the main architects of the genocide, Théoneste Bagosora, had warned of the impending apocalypse before the genocide started. The genocide had been planned well in advance; the death of President Habyarimana was just an excuse. In fact, one of the theories behind the death of Habyarimana is that his plane was shot down by Hutu extremists for two reasons: First he was seen by Hutu extremists as a sell-out because he was negotiating with the RPF in order to have a government of national unity; Second, the death of the president would be used by the hardliners to convince the population that the RPF was responsible, and therefore they (the Hutus) would be justified in killing Tutsis.

In Tanzania, people reacted to the death of Habyarimana with mixed feelings. While some Rwandans celebrated his death, others saw this as bad news because it would lead to more persecution of Tutsi people inside Rwanda. I was of the latter view. In Mwanza, northern Tanzania, some Rwandese who openly celebrated the death of Habyarimana were rounded up by the police and detained. Retired President Nyerere intervened and they were released. He argued that although celebrating the death of a person may be unethical, it is not a criminal offence. As the genocide gained momentum, every person of Rwandese origin in Tanzania was perplexed. We were all worried because, apart from the fact that most of us still had family and friends in Rwanda, the thought of the 'final solution' of killing every Tutsi was really frightening. The RPF stopped the genocide in July 1994 and a new government was put in place. It was led by President Pasteur Bizimungu, a Hutu who had led the RPF negotiating team in Arusha, with Major General Kagame, a Tutsi, as his Vice-President. As soon as the genocide was over, people of Rwandese origin in the diaspora started going back to Rwanda. By mid-1995, most Rwandese in the countries neighbouring Rwanda had gone back home. In Karagwe, members of my family were among those who left for Rwanda. In Dar es Salaam, as well as in many other cities and towns in Tanzania, quite a number of people of Rwandese origin were abandoning their jobs to go back to Rwanda. The new government in Rwanda wanted people who would fill posts needed to run an efficient government because they were starting from the scratch. There was an incentive, especially for educated people, to go back to Rwanda. Personally, I was contacted on several occasions with offers of high ranking posts inside the government and at the National University in Butare. I faced a dilemma: On the one hand, I was already a Tanzanian citizen. Tanzania had raised me and educated me. I had not been to Rwanda for 34 years; I just had very distant memories of my childhood in Rwanda. In any case, I was not very young and I had a family to look after. On the other hand, Rwanda was my motherland; I was still attached to it culturally and I could not deny my origin. It was a very difficult decision to make. Rwanda gave me my heart; Tanzania gave me my brain. I found it difficult to choose between my heart and my brain. In the end, after consultation with my family, I decided I would remain in Tanzania.

From 1994 onwards, the University of Dar es Salaam saw far-reaching changes under the leadership of Prof. Luhanga as Vice-Chancellor. This was the beginning of the transformation programme whose main objective was "to carry out strategic long-term reform that would enable the University to overcome its weaknesses and equip it to meet challenges and fulfil its role in the twenty-first century" (Mkude p.15). Some of these changes included increasing the enrolment of undergraduate students to unprecedented levels. This did not go well with some academic members of staff and students, because it was seen as lowering standards. The argument of the opponents of these changes was that increased enrolment should be subject to availability of facilities such as lecture theatres, student hostels, books, etc. On one occasion, students complained to the Vice-Chancellor that the number of students was too big for the available resources and facilities. The Vice-Chancellor retorted that he was ready to reduce the number of students, so anybody who wanted to be among those to be sent away should come to his office and register themselves. Not a single student took the offer!

Other changes involved negotiations with the government on the need for a more autonomous University, as well as a budget based on student unit cost instead of grants from the government that did not take into consideration the actual cost it takes to educate each student. Within the University, some senior academics complained that the changes were too bureaucratic and that the new governance systems were not transparent and accountable enough. Specifically, these academics wanted University leaders at various levels of the administration to be elected instead of being appointed by University management (Mkude p.15).

It was at the beginning of these far-reaching changes that, I was appointed Head of the Department of Foreign Languages and Linguistics in July 1994, a position I held for six years, until July 2000.

Being Head of Department was not an easy ride. To start with, I had been away from the university for quite a long time, during my studies at Lancaster, so I had been detached from the university environment. I had therefore to acclimatize and learn the 'politics' of the department in particular, and the university in general.

Secondly, when I became Head of Department, there were some factions within the department which I had to try and work with, without being seen to favour one side or the other. For example, going through the files of the department, I realized that two senior colleagues were not on good terms. They had exchanged acrimonious letters, and, as Head of Department, I could see that they were still not on the best of terms. Both of them were my seniors because even when I was an undergraduate student they were already members of staff in the department. However, in terms of academic rank, the three of us were now at the same level of senior lecturer. I had to walk a tight rope to show them that I did not favour one over the other.

In addition, the fact that I became senior lecturer and now Head of Department before some of the colleagues I had found in the department when I was recruited in 1982 was a source of resentment on the part of some of these colleagues. I had to learn to live with them without reciprocating this resentment. I had no reason to dislike them.

I worked under two Deans of the Faculty of Arts and Social Sciences. During the first triennium (1994-1997), I worked under Prof. Munishi, while during the second triennium (1997-2000), I was under Prof.

Mukandala. I had no problem with either of the two deans. The transition from Prof. Munishi to Prof Mukandala was not very smooth. It was rumoured that Prof. Munishi did not want Prof. Mukandala to succeed him, and the former did all in his power to stop the latter from becoming Dean. Although there is no hard evidence to support this, such incidents show the kind of politics going on in public places. Such struggles for power sometimes may put somebody in a position of leadership, or prevent them from accessing that position just because they have the right or wrong connections. In the end, Prof. Mukandala was appointed Dean.

I remember one nasty incident when I was left as Acting Dean while Prof. Mukandala was away. I went to attend a Senate meeting chaired by the Vice-Chancellor, Prof. Luhanga. The Senate meeting was discussing examination results. The results for the Faculty of Arts and Social Sciences were not in the meeting room yet; an administrative officer was finalizing photocopying them. When my turn came, I told the Vice-Chancellor the results would be in soon. He was furious and ordered me out of the room to go and get them. I was so humiliated. My only consolation was I was not the first person to be treated like this. That was Prof. Luhanga's style.

On another occasion when I had been Head of Department for only a few weeks, the Department invited the Permanent Secretary of the Ministry of Higher Education, Dr. Mohamed Gharib Bilal, to officially open an international conference on language and education. The Vice-Chancellor was, by protocol, the host of the Permanent Secretary. When at the end of the ceremony I was called upon to give a vote of thanks to the Guest of Honour in my capacity as Head of Department, my voice was a bit shaky, not being used to such high profile occasions. That did not escape the attention of the Vice-Chancellor. When we were escorting the Permanent Secretary to his car, the driver was a bit unsure in his manoeuvre of the car to the right position. The Vice-Chancellor quipped: he must be trembling because he is not used to driving the Permanent Secretary. I was sure that was meant for me, not the driver!

## Two Key Debates at the University of Dar es Salaam

When I was an undergraduate student, the University of Dar es Salaam was still basking in its glory as the radical Dar es Salaam school of thought, even though it was now on the decline. From the 1960s through the 1970s, academic heavyweights came from different parts of the world to engage in discourse with people like Walter Rodney, Dani

Wadada Nabudere, Mahmood Mamdani, and rising stars like Issa G. Shivji. In those days, both students and academic staff were eager to discuss different issues pertaining to the development of Tanzania and how this was influenced by what was going on elsewhere in the world. When I arrived at the University of Dar es Salaam in 1979, these debates were still going on, especially in the Institute of Development Studies and in the Department of Literature. I have mentioned earlier on people like Grant Kamenju, who believed, and rightly so, that literature cannot be neutral. Literary intellectuals must be engaged in the societies in which they live. Dr. Kamenju was known for playing with words at the expense of "European imperialists", as he called all Western Europeans. He used to say, for example, that Western Europe did not bring technology and civilization to Africa; what they brought was western *tricknology* and *syphilisation*.

However, in the mid-1980s, the trend started to change. The second phase administration under President Mwinyi started the process of the liberalization of the economy because of pressure from the World Bank and the International Monetary Fund (IMF). By the early 1990s, most intellectuals at the University of Dar es Salaam, who had earlier on been staunch Marxists, were now singing the song of the free market and the virtues of a multi-party system. The economists were the first to jump on the band wagon, followed by those from other disciplines. The Institute of Development Studies changed its orientation completely; the only thing that remained the same was the name. To be fair, a few intellectuals on the Hill stuck to their guns. Prof. Issa G. Shivji, the late Prof. Chachage Seth Chachage, the late Prof. Haroub Othman and a few others were completely opposed to the new dispensation driven by the western project of globalization. Playing with the word for globalization in Kiswahili, *utandawazi* (literally, open network), Prof. Chachage used to call globalization *utandawizi*, i.e. a network of thieves. Most other intellectuals were now more interested in undertaking research and consultancies which were driven by Western priorities: globalization, liberalization of the economy, gender issues, poverty alleviation, the environment, etc. The aim was to get quick money, and to be in the good books of Western donors. What is interesting about this period is that even areas that one may see as being beneficial to Tanzania and Africa like environmental issues, gender issues and poverty alleviation were foreign-money driven. These were not priorities identified locally; they were imposed from outside.

I don't like to attach labels to my beliefs, but I have sympathy with those intellectuals who question the current neo-liberal ideology of the west and those African leaders who subscribe to it. What we witness today as liberalism and globalization is, in fact, imperialism in a new form. Old fashioned imperialism depended on guns; modern imperialism (called globalization) depends on markets. The end result is the same: powerful nations exploit the resources of the weak, and within the weak nations there are glaring inequalities between the haves and the have-nots. I also believe cut-throat capitalism without a human face, even within the powerful nations, is doomed to fail, as can be seen from the economic crises in both the United States of America and Western Europe (especially the Euro zone).

The Scandinavian model used to be some kind of middle of the road between socialism and capitalism, in which the welfare system ensured that no one was left to starve. This model, however, is changing as these countries move more and more to the right, even with some groups within these countries moving to the extreme right. I think the Chinese system, which combines free enterprise with government intervention in the economy is much more beneficial to the majority of the people than the *laissez faire* capitalism we see in the West today. I think the problem with most African countries today is that neo-liberalism is not helping African people to benefit from the natural resources that they have in their countries. The so-called Western investors and now the Chinese are only interested in getting Africa's wealth, and the partnerships we enter with them are almost always for their benefit and to our detriment. One would dare to say it is a partnership between a horse and its rider (Moyo 2012).

In my field of specialization, which is linguistics, I have always believed, and still believe, that language and culture are inseparable. I also believe that if people lose or are deprived of their language, they also lose their soul as a people, and cannot have any meaningful development. I have always argued that while we need foreign languages like English, French, Chinese, etc., we cannot have any meaningful development if we ignore our African languages. If we look around the world, no country has ever advanced economically or technologically using a foreign language. Africa cannot be an exception to this rule. Europe started to undergo tremendous social and economic changes that led to the industrial revolution when Europeans cast away Latin and started using their own languages. Martin Luther was a pioneer in that he translated the Bible from Latin into German, demonstrating that

German, and by extension other European languages, were not inferior to Latin.

I have also consistently argued that English Language Teaching (ELT) is big business for the United Kingdom and the United States of America. The politics of ELT in Africa have to be seen within that context. The USA and the UK have an interest in the maintenance of the dominance of English in Africa because of the economic advantages they derive from it: creating jobs for their people who go to different parts of the world as ELT experts; selling books and other language teaching materials to countries where English is taught as a second or foreign language. More importantly, the ELT industry is not only about imparting knowledge and language skills, it is also about influencing the way other people view the world. People don't only read the word, they also read the world. ELT books and materials are not value free; they embody the western, and especially the American, world view.

Within this context, even aid provided by the USA and the UK to African countries ostensibly for promoting the learning of English cannot be neutral. It is part of what Dambisa Moyo, a renowned Zambian economist, has called dead aid (Moyo 2010). ELT projects from the USA and the UK to Africa are always conceived from outside Africa and are donor-driven. It is the donors who set the agenda as to what the priorities should be and how the money should be spent. At the end of the project, there is usually no sustainability of the activities because there is no more money. It is also doubtful if the project activities have any long lasting impact on the quality of education in the recipient country. In Tanzania, for example, the English Language Teaching Support Project (ELTSP) financed by the British Government in the 1980s and 1990s does not seem to have achieved the intended objective, i.e. to improve the standard of English in secondary schools through an extensive reading programme. Nor has a more recent project (2006-2010) funded by the British Department for International Development (DfID) made any impact. This was intended to improve the quality of education through improved English literacy in secondary schools.

In view of my conviction about the importance of African languages for the socio-economic development of Africa, I have always advocated for a change in the medium of instruction from English to Kiswahili in Tanzania, to go hand in hand with the teaching of English as a foreign language. We do not have to engage in a futile debate that is based on a false dichotomy. The question is not whether we should go for **EITHER** English **OR** Kiswahili. We need both. However, we need to understand that, in order to learn English effectively, we do not need to have it as a medium of instruction. What we need is to have well trained teachers of English as a foreign language, who can teach it effectively. Scandinavian countries, for example, teach English as a foreign language, and most Scandinavians are very fluent speakers of English.

The argument that is used for the continued use of English as a medium of instruction in African educational systems is that the world is now a global village, and if we don't use English we will be isolated from this global village. This is a very absurd argument, to say the least. Is China isolated from the global village? No. Do Chinese use English as a medium of instruction in their educational system? No! One could cite examples of other countries that use their own languages and still gain access to the global village. We also tend to forget that the so-called global village is composed of a few very powerful chiefs and many powerless villagers. As mentioned above, ELT benefits the chiefs (USA and UK) and has very little value for the majority of the villagers (the majority of the people in Third World countries).

Some of my work while at the University of Dar es Salaam has contributed to the wider debate regarding language in education in Africa. My work with the Canadian International Development Research Centre (IDRC) contributed to the workshop organized by the late Prof. Neville Alexander at the University of Cape Town, and later to a conference on language in education in Africa convened in Accra, Ghana in 1996. A World Bank consultancy resulted in teaching materials used in different parts of the world (Rubagumya et. Al. 1997; 2000). And in a keynote address I made at the British Association for Applied Linguistics (BAAL) conference in Leeds in 2003 (Rubagumya 2004), I questioned the role of English in enabling Africa to be part of the 'global village.' In all these efforts, I wanted to contribute to the wider debate on English in Africa.

More specifically, in Tanzania, the debate on whether to use English or Kiswahili as a medium of instruction in our secondary schools has been going on for decades now and there is no indication that it will be resolved any time soon. I have, in one way or the other, been involved in this debate in my professional capacity. For example, in 1997/98 I was engaged as a consultant by the Tanzanian Ministry of Education and Culture, alongside with Tanzanian and British colleagues, to look at the role and status of English as a language of teaching and learning in Tanzanian secondary schools, and to make appropriate recommendations on whether or not the status quo should remain, or what changes, if any, should be made. We recommended the strengthening of teaching English as a subject, as well as gradually changing the medium of instruction from English to Kiswahili after adequate preparation of textbooks in Kiswahili and of teachers trained to teach using Kiswahili.

After we had submitted our report, nothing was heard until 1999, when the Director of Culture in the Ministry of Education and Culture set up a committee to work on the details of the transition from English medium to Kiswahili medium secondary education. Again I was asked to be a member of that committee. We did our assignment and submitted the report. I have not heard anything about that report to this day! What I discovered while I was working on the two assignments in the Ministry of Education and Culture is that there were tensions between the two sections of the Ministry: education and culture. People in the education part of the Ministry saw the Directorate of Culture as a peripheral appendage to the Ministry; therefore their views were not always taken seriously. While the Director of Culture, Mr. Ndagara, was enthusiastic about the move to change the medium of instruction, the people in Education 'proper' were dilly dallying about the proposed change. This situation sometimes led to contradictory policies emanating from the same Ministry. For instance, while the *Education and Training Policy* of 1995 stated that English will remain the medium of instruction at secondary level, the *Sera ya Utamaduni* (Cultural Policy) of 1997 from the same Ministry stated that Kiswahili will, after necessary preparations have been made, be the medium of instruction throughout the whole educational system. The fact that the change of the medium of instruction has not yet happened is an outcome of these tensions and contradictions. It is also the outcome of the politics influencing policy decisions behind the scenes. For example, the Ministry of Education Consultancy mentioned above was financed by the British government. Although there is no hard evidence, it would be naïve to think that this assistance had no strings attached.

A British Council officer in Dar es Salaam who controlled the budget for this consultancy did indicate that it was he, not the Ministry of Education, who was in charge. One day I asked him to consider raising my consultancy fee because my British counterpart was getting about three times what I was getting when I was in fact senior to her. The British Council officer said to me arrogantly that he could give me $1000 a day if he wanted, but there would be no change to the rate he had offered me. Obviously, it was not true that he could give me whatever rate he wanted; he was a junior officer and he must have got instructions on what to pay me from his superiors. The point he was making, in a rather rude way, was that this was British money and they did not have to treat the local consultant as equal to the British consultant.

As in the ELTSP project mentioned earlier, the main aim of the British government must have been to ensure the status quo. In a subsequent government reorganization, the Directorate of Culture was removed from the Ministry of Education. Whether or not it was because of these tensions is not clear.

The debate about the language of instruction in Tanzania has always been linked to the quality of the education provided in the country. The proponents of language change from English to Kiswahili argue that it is not possible to provide quality education when both learners and teachers do not have adequate proficiency in the language of instruction. The opponents of the shift to Kiswahili on the other hand, argue that changing the language of instruction will disadvantage Tanzania by isolating the country from the rest of the world. I have shown earlier in this book that such an argument is absurd, to say the least. Unfortunately, this debate has gone on since independence in 1961 and has not been concluded to-date. Over the years, it has generated more heat than light. Since quality education is a prerequisite for socio-economic development, the language issue in Tanzania cannot be excluded from the debates about the development of the country.

Dar es Salaam, Tanzania (1996): Vice-Chancellor of the University of Dar es Salaam, Prof. Mathew Luhanga, opening an international conference on Language Contact, with the author seated right and Prof. René Dirven (Belgium) seated left.

Dar es Salaam, Tanzania (1989): The author's wife, Monica (right), with his Ph.D. supervisor, Prof. Marilyn Martin-Jones.

## Return to Rwanda: 1997

My father and other members of my family left Karagwe and returned to Rwanda in 1995, about one year after the genocide. Of my immediate family, only my mother stayed behind, and this decision was due to ill health. We made arrangements for her to join me in Dar es Salaam.

On 20<sup>th</sup>June 1997, my father died at the age of 81. He had gone back to his "European" house at Nyarubuye. When I got the sad news of my father's death, I flew to Kigali the following day, spent a night with relatives, and the following morning travelled to Nyarubuye. My father was buried in front of his house the very day he died because, as I said earlier, there are no facilities for treating the dead in the village.

The only thing I could do was to pay my last respects at the grave. Because of my arrival, the family also took the opportunity to discuss family matters, especially deciding on who should now be the head of the family after my father's death. That was easy, because it is the eldest son who takes over the responsibilities of the family in such circumstances. Therefore it was unanimously agreed that my brother Louis would become the head of the family. Matters of my late father's estate were also decided at that meeting.

One thing that struck me on my return to the village after 36 years of absence was how everything had shrunk in size and distance. The family house I had left behind seemed extremely small compared to my mental recollection of what it had been like in1961 when we left. Even the distances to neighbours' houses and to the Catholic Church from my childhood home looked much shorter than they had to a child's eyes. The visit to the Catholic Church was the greatest shock of my life. As mentioned in chapter one, this was a place where some of the most gruesome atrocities had been committed during the genocide. Although the church itself had been cleaned and was in use, dead bodies were scattered all over the place in what had been the nunnery and the primary school. Most of them had not been properly buried. I was told that this was intended to be one of the genocide memorial sites, so these bodies were deliberately left unburied. Apparently arrangements were being made to treat whatever remains of the bodies there were. Dry blood stains could be seen on all walls. I was told horrifying stories of babies whose heads were banged on walls, splitting their skulls and splashing their brains all over the place. I found it very difficult to understand how a human being could do such a thing to an innocent baby.

The killing at Nyarubuye had begun by attacking the Tutsi at the local marketplace. Many of them ran to the Catholic Church, believing it to be safe. They were mistaken. The local mayor, Sylvestre Gacumbitsi, led a group of *interahamwe* to the church. They first asked people to hand over their money, saying they would spare those who paid. After taking the money, they killed them all the same. They threw hand grenades into the church. They smashed people's heads with nailed clubs or with stones, saying they were killing snakes, and you kill a snake by smashing its head. Babies were snatched from their mothers and plunged into open pit latrines, head first. Women were gang raped before they were killed; pregnant women were cut open. The killing took place over a period of four days. At night the killers rested, guarding the church to ensure nobody escaped. Some people survived by hiding among the corpses (PBS).

While in Rwanda, I took the opportunity to visit some institutions of higher learning, just for curiosity to see how they were coping with the challenges of post-genocide education. I had been approached before by the National University of Rwanda (NUR) in Butare and the Kigali Institute of Science and Technology (KIST), both asking me whether I would be willing to work for them. I had refused both offers, but said I would be willing to do some short term assignments with them. This time, since I happened to be in Rwanda, I wanted to pursue the idea further.

At the National University of Rwanda, they offered me a short term contract of one semester to teach linguistics courses. I said I would consider the offer. When I returned to Tanzania, I asked for time off from the University of Dar es Salaam to go and undertake this assignment. The Chief Academic Officer, Prof. Penina Mlama, refused, citing two reasons: first, I was Head of the Department of Foreign Languages and Linguistics. As Head of Department, I could not leave, especially since the timing coincided with the beginning of the new academic year. Secondly, the University of Dar es Salaam did not have any cooperation agreement with the National University of Rwanda. Even though these reasons were plausible, I suspected there might have been another non- stated reason that influenced the decision of the Chief Academic Officer. During the period immediately after the genocide, many people of Rwandese origin who had taken up Tanzanian citizenship were leaving their jobs in Tanzania to go and take up new jobs in Rwanda. At the University of Dar es Salaam, for instance, a renowned economist, Dr. Laurian Rutayisire, who was a member of the Board of the Bank of Tanzania, left surreptitiously to take up the job of Deputy Governor of the Central Bank of Rwanda.

Around this time, former Rwandese refugees who had been granted citizenship of Tanzania were in a catch 22 situation. You were damned if you returned to Rwanda and you were damned if you didn't. If you returned, you were accused of being ungrateful to the country which had given you refuge for many years and granted you citizenship. If you did not go back to Rwanda, you were accused of taking up jobs meant for Tanzanians. Many Tanzanians of Rwandese origin faced the same dilemma as me. Should they go back to Rwanda or should they stay? In some cases there were even disagreements in the same family, which led to some members of the family going back to Rwanda and others staying in Tanzania.

My employer might have thought that I was also on my way out, and that this request was just camouflage to get me out of the country. However, I had no such intention. If I had wanted to go for good, I would have told my employer the truth. In any case, refusing me permission to be away for one semester would not have prevented me from leaving, if my aim had been to go back to work in Rwanda permanently. I therefore accepted my employer's decision and told the National University of Rwanda that I was unable to take up the offer.

Towards the end of 1997,the Kigali Institute of Science and Technology (KIST) asked me to undertake for them a short term consultancy which involved preparing language curricula (English and French). The linguistic situation in Rwanda after the genocide was interesting. People had come from different corners of the world, speaking different languages. The majority of the returnees were from Tanzania, Kenya, Uganda (Anglophone); Burundi and the Democratic Republic of the Congo (Francophone). The one million dollar question therefore was: which language should be used as the medium of instruction at the different levels of education? For KIST and the National University of Rwanda, the solution was bilingualism: every student should learn both English and French; lecturers would give lectures in their preferred language, either English or French, depending on whether they are Anglophone or Francophone; hence the need for KIST to have curricula for the two languages. I undertook the assignment and submitted my recommendations in January 1998.

In 2008, the government of Rwanda decided to abolish French as a medium of instruction and replaced it with English, without really much preparation. The justification for this change was that Rwanda was closer to East Africa, which was "Anglophone", than to the "Francophone" block of West Africa. Rwanda was also in the process of applying for membership in the Commonwealth, again an "Anglophone" club. However, it is believed in many circles that the main reason for this shift was the misunderstanding between Rwanda and France. Rwanda had accused France of being behind the genocide of 1994, while France had, on her part, accused President Kagame of killing former President Habyarimana, whose plane was shot down as it was approaching Kigali airport on 6th April 1994. At one point, things were so bad between Rwanda and France that diplomatic relations were suspended in 2006.

## A Recommitment to Tanzania in the New Millennium

In 2000, as the new millennium began, I was faced with an offer and two death threats which caused me to re-evaluate my commitment to Tanzania. In the end, I chose again to reaffirm my life as a citizen of Tanzania.

In 2000, I was approached by the Department of Language Education of the Faculty of Education at the University of Botswana, asking me if I would be willing to be considered for a position of Senior Lecturer in the Department. I had been External Examiner in the Department for three years from 1997 to 1999. Around this time, quite a number of academic staff from Tanzanian universities, as well as other professionals, were going to Botswana in search of greener pastures. The package proposed to me was very tempting, so I really agonized over whether I should accept that offer or not. In the end, I declined for two main reasons. First, I was staying with my mother, who was 85 years old. If I accepted the offer, the family would have to relocate to Botswana. There was no way we could take my mother with us at that age, and there was no other place where we would leave her. Second, I had heard stories of xenophobia in Botswana, and I had no intention of being a 'refugee' for the second time.

As it turned out, my mother died in May 2000, just a few weeks after I declined the University of Botswana offer. Just before my mother died, my wife and I had a car accident. Fortunately, we escaped without any injury, but the car was badly damaged. When my mother died, my wife told me the car accident had been a harbinger of the death of my mother. I did not believe her, but maybe she was right, I simply don't know.

My mother was buried in Dar es Salaam because that is where most of the members of the family were. Only my brother Louis came from Rwanda for the funeral. With the death of my mother, just three years after the death of my father, the old generation of my parents was now gone and we in the family were on our own. I remember one cousin of mine who said at the funeral that she hoped the passing of our parents would not bring about the disintegration of the family, because they were the ones holding us together. Fortunately, this has not happened.

Another event that happened in 2000 and that I vividly remember was the death of a cousin of mine, Gaetan Zimulinda, who was a pastor of the Baptist Church in Dar es Salaam. Pastor Zimulinda was murdered by a group of unknown persons in front of his wife and three children. The assailants invaded his home in Boko on the outskirts of Dar es Salaam in the evening. They first beat him with clubs and stones; he tried his best to struggle and defend himself, but the group overpowered him. After beating him, they finished him off by shooting him in the head. They did not steal anything from the house, so obviously these were not robbers; they had come specifically to kill the pastor. To this day, no one has ever been arrested in connection with this murder.

One month after the murder of Pastor Zimulinda, somebody phoned me at my home on the university campus using my home landline. He spoke English with a heavy West African accent. He said he was behind the killing of Pastor Zimulinda and he deeply regretted it. He also said I was not safe in Dar es Salaam and I should seriously consider leaving the city for my safety. He immediately hung up. I reported this call to the police station at the university. They took my statement, and that was it. Obviously, my family and I were very concerned, but we decided to wait and see.

A few weeks later, we had just retired to bed when our son Safari shouted from the living room. He had remained in the living room studying, while the rest of us went to bed. Then suddenly, he saw one of the curtains on fire. He struggled to put the fire out, while shouting for help. When we came down, he had already managed to extinguish the fire. We called our neighbours and immediately reported the incident to the police station. A police officer came to the scene the same night. It was obvious the fire had been started from outside. Again we made statements, but as in the previous incidents, no one has ever been arrested for this crime.

It is very tempting to link the death of Pastor Zimulinda, the telephone call and the attempted arson. However, in the absence of any arrests, it is really very difficult to know the truth of the matter. The question will always be: why was Pastor Zimulinda killed? There are two theories. One is that he was killed by Hutu extremists or their agents as part of their grand project of the "final solution", i.e. killing all the Tutsi wherever they are. The second theory is that Pastor Zimulinda was killed by people he had dealings with, either people within his church or outside the church. The first theory is difficult to sustain. Pastor Zimulinda was not the only Tutsi in Dar es Salaam or in Tanzania for that matter. To the best of my knowledge, no other Tutsi had been killed before in Dar, and none has been killed in such suspicious circumstances since the death of the pastor. So why should he be the only one targeted? The second theory is more plausible. If he was killed by his personal enemies, for whatever reason, the link with the anonymous telephone call and the attempted arson makes more sense. If somebody wanted to kill me, as intimated in the telephone call, they would not have warned me to leave Dar es Salaam. These are people who knew that I was a close relative to Pastor Zimulinda, so they probably wanted me to panic and leave Dar es Salaam so that I do not follow up the case. When I did not leave, they devised another tactic to further intimidate me, the attempted arson. I must say that even this latter scenario, in the absence of any evidence, just remains an assumption of what might have happened. The truth will probably remain buried with my cousin and the people who committed this crime.

With the death of my mother, I could have reconsidered taking the offer at the University of Botswana because there was no obstacle now to our going there. The two death threats to me and my family also increased my feelings of insecurity in Tanzania at that time. However, in the end I decided to stay put in Tanzania. I had to take a calculated risk. Somehow I felt that the death threats were meant to intimidate me into leaving Dar es Salaam, rather than being intended to be real threats to my life or the lives of my family. With hind sight, I was right because I stayed in Dar es Salaam for another eight years and nothing happened to me or to my family.

## Reflections on Being Director of Student Services

After being Head of Department, I was appointed Associate Dean for Academic Affairs in the Faculty of Arts and Social Sciences. After serving only six months, I was appointed Director of Student Services. At this time, Prof. Amandina Lihamba was the Dean of the Faculty and Prof. Makenya Maboko was the Director of Undergraduate Studies, the two posts I had also been shortlisted for.

An incident that I remember vividly as Director of Student Services is when I was summoned to Dodoma by the Vice-Chancellor, Prof. Mathew Luhanga, in the middle of the night. Prof. Luhanga phoned me at around 9pm and asked me why I had not accompanied the Dar es Salaam University Students Organization (DARUSO) leaders to Dodoma to meet the minister responsible for Higher Education, Dr. Ng'wandu. Both the minister and the vice-chancellor were in Dodoma. Although I explained that the DARUSO leaders had not told me they intended to go to Dodoma to meet the minister, he said that was no excuse for me not to be in Dodoma! The meeting with the minister was scheduled the following morning at8am and he expected me to be there. When I told him I would try to be there, he said "you better be there". I understood what that meant. I immediately phoned my driver, who stayed at Kitunda, and told him we had to be in Dodoma by 8am. We agreed he would pick me up at 1am on campus and we would start our journey to Dodoma. He was at my house on the dot. My instructions to the driver were: be fast but careful. Fortunately, there was very little traffic at that time of the night and we arrived safely at Dodoma at 7:30am.

The meeting with the minister, of course, started not at 8am as scheduled, but at 10:00am. Once it was underway, it turned out to be a one man show. After the DARUSO leaders had told the minister why they had asked to meet him, he started a long lecture, telling them to be good boys and girls and not to listen to people who wanted to distract them from their primary duty, which is studying. Neither the vice-chancellor nor I had any opportunity to make any contribution to the meeting.

After the meeting, the vice-chancellor invited me and the student leaders to lunch at Dodoma Hotel. After lunch I told the driver we would drive back and spend a night in Morogoro to give ourselves time to rest. We drove to Dar es Salaam the following day. As I was going back, I wondered whether the journey was worth it. Apart from protocol considerations, was it really necessary for me to spend a sleepless night just in order to be present at the meeting?

But my tenure as Director of Student Services (later re-changed to Dean of Students) did give me insights into student behaviour that I had not been able to get in all the years I had been teaching, both at secondary and university levels (Rubagumya 2010). The position led me to think deeply about whether university students should be considered adults or children, as well as to consider the effects of limited financial resources on both the education environment and student behaviour, to try to find better parameters for student leadership, and to understand the impact of globalization on student behaviour.

In the early days of university education in Tanzania, students were fully dependent on the government for their education and upkeep. This support included fees (in the form of government bursaries), accommodation and meals, health services, and a small stipend for incidental expenses. Total dependence on government support implied that university students were in a paternalistic relationship with the government, and through it, the university administration. The "benevolent" government provided for the students, who in return were expected to be "obedient children".

With the introduction of cost sharing in the early 1990s, students were expected to meet some of their education expenses. Because of this change, students were expected to be more responsible persons in terms of finding ways and means of partially meeting the cost of their education. The philosophy guiding student affairs had therefore to change, taking cognizance of the new reality on the ground. Instead of being "obedient children" dependent on a "benevolent" government, students were now expected to be mature, responsible people.

This philosophy on student affairs is premised on two main assumptions: a) that university students are adults; and b) that because they are adults they can behave responsibly. Therefore, instead of being paternalistic towards them, university management should give them opportunities to participate in university governance. The University of Dar es Salaam has therefore, over the years, endeavoured to include student representation in statutory and non-statutory organs of the university. This approach is the same with respect to the University of Dodoma. The organs in which students are represented include Faculty/ School Boards, Senate, Student Affairs Committee and Council.

We might, however, ask ourselves whether all university students are adults and whether it is realistic to assume that they will always behave as responsible adults. From the legal point of view, all persons aged 18 and above are adults. As **most** university students are 18 and above, they are adults. Having said that, the new trend is that we have younger people now coming to university than in the past. It is possible to have 17 year olds being admitted into first year. So it is possible that we might have a few students who are not adults even from the legal point of view.

However, legal adulthood is different from what I would call "common sense adulthood" or acting in a mature way. In the family setting, would you consider your 18 year old son/daughter an adult or a child? If you consider them children, would it then be realistic to assume that all university students are adults? Maybe there is a mismatch between the perception of universities and that of parents vis-a-vis the adulthood of students. We have seen parents doing for their children who are university students things that one would usually expect an adult person to do for himself/ herself. This assistance includes accompanying their children to university on admission into first year, filling out their registration forms, even looking for jobs for their children after graduation! This situation is certainly different from some years back, when students were being admitted to university after National Service, or even after working for at least two years after Form Six during the times of the Musoma Resolution (1974). This resolution was part of Nyerere's implementation of the policy of *Education for Self-Reliance* (ESR), as part of the *Arusha Declaration's* blueprint for a socialist society. It was meant to give prospective university students an opportunity to work before coming to the university. In this way, it was envisaged that they would be more down- to-earth and less elitist in their outlook. However, it is doubtful whether this objective was really achieved. In fact, for girls it turned out to be counter-productive because quite a number of them got pregnant or married in the intervening two years. This ended their dream of getting a university education.

It seems that universities have been rather over-optimistic in their belief that all university students are adults. As will be seen later, some university students have not demonstrated that they behave responsibly as adults. This is not to say that all university students are children, or that they all behave in a childish manner. Quite a good number of them are indeed adults who behave responsibly.

What is needed, in my view, is to engage students in the participatory governance structures of universities, but in a manner that emphasizes mentoring and guidance from university management and faculty. Indeed, where this has been done, we have seen positive results.

Despite efforts at inclusivity over the years when I was Director of Student Services at the University of Dar es Salaam, and indeed later when I moved to the University of Dodoma, I have been witness to a number of crises. I found that these crises were not necessarily tied to the question of student maturity. The main cause of these crises was, in fact, underfunding.

Inadequate funding by the government for public Higher Education Institutions (HEIs) and by the owners of private HEIs led to deteriorating conditions in student hostels in terms of overcrowding and lack of maintenance of accommodation facilities over the years. Similarly, the non-conducive learning and teaching environment is mainly due to inadequate funding for the expansion of infrastructure (lecture rooms, theatres, laboratories, etc.), as well as very little recurrent expenditure funding provided for the day to day running of these institutions.

All these problems related to underfunding are potential causes of student crises, and indeed they have been, at one time or another, the cause of a number of crises. For example, lack of water was one of the main causes of the crisis at Mabibo Hostel, University of Dar es Salaam, in February 2008.

In recent years, inadequate management of student loans by the Higher Education Student Loans Board (HESLB) has been the main cause of student crises. This was the case, for example, of a class boycott by students in the College of Education at the University of Dodoma in March 2009. Their main complaint was that the HESLB had been late in disbursing their loan money.

The impact of restricted finances can also been seen in how students don't want to buy books. They think they can find answers for everything on the internet (Wikipedia). They would rather spend their book allowance on expensive mobile phone hand- sets and music equipment. Because they don't buy books, they either steal books from the university library or vandalize them by tearing pages from them. Students have, for a long time, resisted depositing their book allowance in the university bookshop.

Restricted finances may be one reason, but it is not the only one. Another, maybe more important reason, has to do with the student mind-set and what they see as their priorities. Definitely, if students can afford to buy expensive mobile phone handsets, they can afford to buy some books.

No doubt the internet is a good source of academic materials, but most students don't take trouble to look for these materials by consulting library staff who can provide guidance. The Wikipedia becomes for them just a shortcut to ready-made answers to their questions. The "wikipedia syndrome" is a manifestation of a deeper problem; students have, from their primary and secondary school experiences, been tuned to studying **in order to pass examinations**. Anything that does not contribute to passing examinations is therefore not important for them. So if you can get a ready answer from Wikipedia (or from stolen and vandalized books), why "waste" your money on buying books? This, in my view, is a very serious problem that needs a solution.

Weak and unsustainable student leadership has also been one of the main causes of student crises. There are several aspects to this problem. First, in several HEIs there is no culture of smooth handing over of leadership from one student government to the next. This often has to do with misappropriation of funds by86 outgoing leaders. The outgoing leaders do not hand over files to the in-coming leaders because the former are not in a position to account for the expenditure during their tenure of office. The incoming leadership therefore find no records of expenditure and no money in the account. They in turn do more or less the same thing with the money they get during their term of office. This means the office of the Dean of Students has to sometimes give them a subsidy to allow them to carry out their functions.

The time of change-over of leadership was the worst time. Campaigns were always rough, especially for women who aspired to be student leaders. They were harassed by their male counterparts, and this led many female students to shy away from presenting themselves as candidates. This effect was unfortunate as it led to student leadership which was male dominated and capable women did not get the chance to be leaders. Some students came to campaign meetings drunk, and they made these meetings unmanageable and meaningless. On the polling day, I and staff in my office had to spend a whole day and a sleepless night supervising the poll and the counting of ballot papers. There were always accusations and counter-accusations of election rigging by contesting candidates and their supporters. I remember one such night the situation was so rough that some students attempted to force me out of the room where counting of ballot papers was going on, accusing me of favouring one candidate. This was of course untrue. Security had to intervene to calm the situation.

Second, there is poor communication between student leaders and their fellow students. Although students are represented in various decision-making organs of HEIs, their representatives often do not give any feedback on important decisions affecting students. This lack of communication leads to student complaints that decisions are made without taking their (student) interests into account.

Third, during election campaigns, candidates for various posts try to convince the electorate that they are able to solve all student problems if elected. However, these unrealistic promises give students false hopes. Once they are elected, the leaders are under pressure to deliver on their promises. This in turn leads student leaders to present unrealistic demands to the management of higher education institutions. This situation is a recipe for conflict.

Fourth, student governments usually last for only one year. Such short terms make leadership unsustainable because there is not enough time to put in place a programme of action and see it through. Furthermore, student leaders want to achieve as much as possible in this short period of time, sometimes with disastrous consequences.

Last but not least, there is influence of party politics and other external players on student politics. During campaigns, different political parties want to influence the outcome of campus elections because they want to create constituencies within the student population. There are stories of "big money" from political parties to student candidates in order to influence the outcome of the elections. This kind of interference with campus politics does have a negative effect on how student leaders discharge their duties because, in such a case, student leaders have more allegiance to their sponsors than to fellow students. I know of DARUSO leaders who, after completing their university studies at the University of Dar es Salaam, got leadership positions in political parties. Admittedly, there is no direct evidence that they were given money by political parties when they were student leaders. It is, however, indicative of the possibility of such corruption.

Aspects of globalization, especially the internet, constitute one of the reasons for the changing patterns of behaviour of Tanzanian students in HEIs. The influence of the internet, especially access to pornographic material by students, has led to more liberal attitudes towards sex. Some students imitate what they see on the internet by engaging in group and/ or public sex, and generally not seeing any problem with what would normally be seen as taboo in Tanzanian society (e.g. homosexual/ lesbian practices). It is suggested that materialism and individualism, which are part of the ethos of globalization, have influenced some students in looking for money and material goods at any cost. Thus, some female students are said to engage in sexual relationships because of the material benefits that accrue from these relationships, in the form of the so-called 3 Cs (car, cash, cell phone).

Another influence of Western liberalism on university students is in connection with alcohol and drug abuse. The number of students involved in this behaviour may not be big, but it is "normal" in the sense that most students know that there are fellow students who get drunk and/or abuse drugs. The significance of alcohol and drug abuse is not in the numbers, but in the damage it causes to those involved. It is also an anti-social behaviour because, when these few students get drunk and/ or smoke marijuana, they become a nuisance to their fellow students.

Dress code has for some time now been an issue in a number of universities in Tanzania. In several universities, this issue is something that has always been discussed, but so far no solution has been found. The problem, as it is presented, is that some students dress in a way that is "not acceptable to society". But this in itself begs a number of questions: what is acceptable and what is not acceptable? Who decides that some ways of dressing are acceptable while others are not? Should we, or should we not, as university managers, prescribe a dress code for our students? If we do so, is this not encroaching on individual human rights? Some universities have embarked on a dialogue with students on self-monitoring in terms of what dress practices are acceptable to the community. This approach seems to have worked quite well without having to impose a strict dress code, which would in any case be difficult to enforce.

The period between 1994 and 2008 was for me a period of growth, both academically and in terms of university leadership experience. After my Ph.D. at Lancaster University I was engaged in all the three key functions of a university: teaching, research and consultancy work.

My main field of competence and interest was, and still is, the interface between language and education.

Over the years, my activities in these key functions have made my conviction that language is a necessary, though not sufficient, condition to achieving quality education even stronger.

As far as university leadership is concerned, my experience as Head of Department, Associate Dean and Director of Student Services was very rewarding, but also very challenging. It was rewarding because I had an opportunity to make a small contribution to the growth of the University of Das es Salaam.

At the same time, it was challenging because it is not easy to forge unity of purpose among people of diverse interests and character. Being Director of Student Services was particularly challenging because student expectations are often unrealistic and they can therefore make your job quite stressful.

It was during this period that I also had the dilemma of whether or not I should go back to Rwanda after the 1994 genocide. I decided to stay in Tanzania, although I actually had good reasons for going to Rwanda, including the probability of getting a high profile job and the threats to my life after the death of my cousin, Reverend Zimulinda.

As things turned out, in 2008 I was to start a new chapter of my life, this time at the newly established University of Dodoma.

Chapter Five

# The University of Dodoma

## Challenges Faced by a New University

I completed my tenure as Director of Student Services/Dean of Students at the University of Dar es Salaam in April 2008. My tenure was supposed to be over in December 2007, but my replacement had not been appointed on time. When Dr. Martha Qorro was finally appointed, in April 2008, I went back to the Department of Foreign Languages and Linguistics to do the job I was employed to do in the first place: full time teaching, research and consultancy. By this time, I had already reached the age of compulsory retirement at 60, so I had, from December 2006, been working on contract terms.

After working in the Department for a couple of months, I was approached by an emissary sent by the University of Dodoma to ask me whether I was willing to be considered for a position as principal of one of the colleges. The University of Dodoma had just been established the previous year and I knew very little about it. I told the emissary that I was already a retired professor working on contract terms. He said the University of Dodoma was looking for somebody who was not yet retired, so we bade each other goodbye, and, as far as I was concerned, that was the end of the story.

One week later, the same emissary came back to me and said the University of Dodoma would, after all, consider my candidature if I was interested, my retirement status notwithstanding. I agreed and he said he would get back to me in due course. A few days later he called me to arrange an interview. I was called for the interview on 23rd June, 2008 in Dar es Salaam, where I was grilled for about one and a half hours by a very high powered panel of three interviewers. I later learnt that there were three of us being interviewed for the position of Principal, College of Humanities and Social Sciences. After the interview, I went back to my daily activities at the University of Dar es Salaam. I had mixed feelings about the possibility of moving from Dar es Salaam to Dodoma. On the one hand, the fact that the University of Dodoma had shown interest in me, even as a retired professor, meant they thought I could make a contribution. On the other hand, I was not keen on moving to a new place at my age, especially when that place was Dodoma. I guess I had my own prejudices against Dodoma.

I was formally appointed Principal, College of Humanities and Social Sciences of the University of Dodoma by the Chancellor, Hon. Benjamin William Mkapa vide his letter, as relayed to me by the Vice-Chancellor, Prof. Idris Kikula, vide his letter. I took up my new position on 1st October, 2008. By this time I had completed my two year contract with the University of Dar es Salaam, so there was no problem as far as my obligations with the employer were concerned.

Settling down in Dodoma was not easy at first. My family and I found the environment rather hostile. Being a semi-arid area with very low humidity, the first problem one encounters settling in Dodoma is skin care. Your skin becomes very dry. When we came in October 2008, it was the dry season, which stretches from May to November. My son Oscar (13 years old at that time) wondered why I had decided to move to Dodoma from Dar es Salaam. Although he did not say it explicitly, he must have thought I was crazy, leaving a big city to come and live in the wilderness. Looking back, I have no regrets. I now prefer the Dodoma wilderness to the Dar es Salaam wilderness of traffic jams, where one can easily spend a whole hour on the road to move only one kilometre.

I guess any environment is habitable; it all depends on your mind-set. The retired Catholic Bishop of Dodoma, the Rt. Rev. Joseph Isuja, once told me that he disagrees with people who think Dodoma is a hostile place to live in. He said the problem with many people is that they always focus on the negative instead of the positive. He said for him Dodoma is the 'promised land' with plenty of milk and honey. Indeed, Dodoma may be a 'semi-desert', but that desert is fertile.

The University of Dodoma is a show case of what the government can do if there is political will. When I took up my position, all the activities were taking place at Chimwaga building, which was the only facility when the university started in 2007. Student hostels at the College of Humanities and Social Sciences were at the finishing stage, but the contractor had to work 7days a week, 24 hours a day in order to get the hostels ready for the 2008/2009 student intake. Indeed, he met the deadline, so when the first year students came, five blocks of hostels were ready for occupation. Five years on (at the time of writing), the University of Dodoma campus is probably the biggest in Africa and one of the most beautiful I have ever seen. What is more impressive is that not a single cent from outside the country was put into building this university. All the money was provided by social security funds with the government guarantee, in which the latter guaranteed the former that they would be paid back over a specified period of time. The College of Humanities and Social Sciences was built by the National Social Security Fund (NSSF) in two phases. Phase I built the School of Social Sciences, while phase II built the School of Humanities.

The establishment of the University of Dodoma has engendered a lot of disapproval, and at times outright hostility, from both inside and outside the country. The so-called donor community, especially Western countries, has openly opposed the building of a new university in Tanzania, arguing that Tanzania does not need a new university; that the priority for a developing country like Tanzania should be to strengthen primary education. One wonders how a country can develop just by depending on primary school leavers. No wonder we are told that what we need is poverty alleviation, instead of poverty eradication. To me, poverty alleviation sounds like giving a patient a pain killer to alleviate the symptoms of the disease instead of diagnosing and treating the disease itself. It is not possible to eradicate poverty without a critical mass of highly educated people in the different spheres of the national economy. For the West, what Africa needs is to continue its dependence on Western aid for poverty alleviation. The opposition to building a new university in Tanzania can be understood within the context of this Western conception of Africa's role in the world economy.

Tanzania has the lowest university enrolment per capita even within the East African region. One just wonders where the thousands of students now studying at the University of Dodoma would be, had it not been for the decision to establish this new university. Sometimes we forget that providing university education is not only to produce job seekers; it should be especially to produce job creators. In any case, an educated citizen is better than an uneducated one. All things being equal, an educated citizen is bound to do things better and to have a better understanding of the natural and social world surrounding him/her. I think the strange happenings we are witnessing in Tanzania today, like killing albinos (for their body parts) as a short cut to getting rich, bears testimony to how lack of education can plunge us into national calamities.

Internally, the establishment of the University of Dodoma was opposed by other public universities, because it was perceived as a competitor for the meagre resources from the government. Even today, there is a misconception that the University of Dodoma is favoured by the government and gets a disproportionate amount of funds. This is not true. In fact, the University of Dodoma gets much less if you take into consideration the student population. Some universities are smaller than, for instance, the College of Humanities and Social Sciences alone. Yet each of these small universities gets more or less the same amount of subvention from the government as the whole University of Dodoma with six colleges.

It is further alleged from different quarters that the University of Dodoma was a political decision taken by the ruling party, CCM *(Chama Cha Mapinduzi)*, in order to bolster its popularity. This may be true, but all decisions made by governments are political decisions, and in normal circumstances, all governments make decisions that will bolster their popularity. So there is nothing out of the ordinary here. Any ruling party would have made a decision that would have been judged to be in the party's interest, and other parties would not have necessarily liked that decision.

Being a principal in a newly established university was not easy. During the early days, we had challenges with the physical infrastructure: classrooms, offices, library, hostels, roads etc. However, as days went by, this was the easiest challenge to overcome because construction work was going on all the time. We saw buildings mushrooming all over the place. Getting academic staff was, in fact, the biggest challenge. When I came, most academic staff in the college, as indeed in other colleges in the university, were tutorial assistants and assistant lecturers. There were very few members of senior staff. We had therefore to rely on part-time lecturers from outside, mainly from the University of Dar es Salaam, Mzumbe University and Sokoine University of Agriculture. This short term strategy was put in place by the university to overcome this challenge of shortage of academic staff. The other strategy was to recruit academic staff from outside the country. So, lecturers were recruited from India, Russia, Kenya and Nigeria, to mention a few countries.

Recruiting academic staff from India and Russia was controversial. Some people asked, why India and Russia? Why not, for instance, the USA and the UK? After all, Tanzania is an 'Anglophone' country, and Indians and Russians don't speak English well, it was argued. First of all, I find the label 'Anglophone' for Tanzania a misnomer. Only about 5% of Tanzanians can speak English, and the levels of proficiency vary widely even for these 5%. I don't think that, on average, Tanzanians speak better English than Indians or Russians. It is true that accent can be a problem when interacting with Indians and Russians for the first time, but after a while one gets used to the accent. Moreover, the problem of accent is universal. Even other people find it difficult to understand Tanzanian accent, and they probably find it even more difficult to understand British and American accents! The Russian and Indian professors recruited to teach at the University of Dodoma are as good as any in the world. Moreover, they are much cheaper to recruit than those from the USA and Western Europe. However, recruiting academic staff from outside Tanzania is a short-term strategy. In the long run, the university has to train young newly recruited staff to attain Masters degrees and Ph.D.s.

Managing part-time lecturers was one of my biggest headaches as Principal of the College. First, these were not very easy to get because there are many universities and not enough senior academics around. Secondly, even when we got them, it was difficult to ensure they delivered value for the money we paid them. Some would come and compress their teaching into a few days, such that a semester (15 weeks) course would be taught in say only two or three weeks.

Paying part-timers was another challenge. Usually after teaching, part-timers would expect to be paid their money. It was on many occasions not possible to pay them on time because the college did not have money every time a part-time lecturer wanted to be paid. While some understood, others held the college at ransom by withholding student examination results as a way of putting pressure on the college administration to pay them.

Because of shortage of senior academic staff, academic departments were mainly run by junior staff of the rank of assistant lecturer. Although most of these young men and women who were entrusted with these positions were very hard working and diligent, they lacked experience in university management.

Lack of qualified staff sometimes brought the college management into conflict with academic staff on post. One such incident was when one economics lecturer, Mr. Sanga, was asked to teach a course. Because he was on study leave, he said he would teach the course on condition that he be given extra payment over and above his salary. To make things even worse, he inflated the number of hours he was supposed to teach so as to be given more money. The Head of Department and the Dean brought the case to me. It was towards the end of the semester and this course had to be taught. I called the lecturer to my office and tried to reason with him, but he was adamant. He also was very rude to me. I became angry and wrote him a very strong letter demanding he give cause why disciplinary action should not be taken against him. His response to the letter was not satisfactory and the tone of the letter was still very rude and unrepentant. I had no other option but to report this matter to the Deputy Vice-Chancellor (Planning, Finance and Administration) for disciplinary action. Mr. Sanga later, on advice of the Vice-Chancellor, came to apologize to me when he realized that I was not bluffing. He did teach the course and was not given any extra payment. Despite this apology, which was obviously meant to save him from disciplinary action, he was written a strong warning letter by the Chairperson of the Staff Disciplinary Committee. Sadly, this lecturer was not alone in attempting to take advantage of the university's challenging situation. Quite a number of young lecturers displayed the same attitude of wanting extra payment for many of the tasks that they were expected to do by virtue of their employment.

As would be expected of a new university, it was not only human resources that were in short supply, even getting adequate financial resources was a big challenge. In a situation like this, management/staff relations are prone to misunderstandings. Sometimes staff would be impatient because of the not so conducive working environment. Young people were especially impatient, and this led to complaints and rumour mongering that the administration both at the college and university level was not interested in the welfare of the workers. Leaders of the University of Dodoma Academic Staff Assembly (UDOMASA) were very vocal in claiming their right to be paid their different dues on time without trying to understand the difficult circumstances in which the university was operating. One such leader in the College of Humanities and Social Sciences said openly that she was working at UDOM for money; that was what was important for her. That kind of a leader is obviously not very helpful.

Such strains in the staff relations were exacerbated by perceptions, Unjustified in my view, that the university management favoured Muslims at the detriment of Christians. Since both the Vice-Chancellor and the Deputy Vice-Chancellor (Planning, Finance and Administration) were Muslims, some people saw this as 'evidence' of Muslims dominating the university. What these people conveniently forgot was that the other Deputy Vice-Chancellor (Academic) was a Christian, as were all six college principals and the majority of the deans. As of 2012, over 70% of all staff at the university was made up of Christians. So, it was in fact Christians who constituted the dominant religion, not the Muslims.

I can only guess why these rumours of Muslim dominance at the university persisted. A number of senior officers under the Deputy Vice-Chancellor (Planning Finance and Administration) were Muslims. This was the case of the Bursar, the Director of Human Resource and Administration, as well as the Chief Supplies Officer. Unfortunately, these three and one academic member of staff (also a Muslim), who was apparently being groomed to eventually take over from Deputy Vice-Chancellor (Planning, Finance and Administration) (DVCPFA), were on many occasions found in his office as a group. These meetings were probably harmless, but for many people they might have been taken as evidence of a conspiracy to turn the university into a pro-Islamic institution. Usually people make conclusions from what is observable, not from people's intentions, which are hard to discover. That is why it is said justice must not only be done; it must also BE SEEN TO BE DONE. So when people found the quartet drinking coffee with the DVCPFA almost on a daily basis, it was tempting to believe they were up to some mischief.

At one time, suspicions of religious discord were so rampant that the University Workers Council decided to appoint a committee to investigate these allegations. I was appointed Chairperson of this Committee. The committee was unable to do the job because, even within the committee, we did not trust each other. One member of the committee, a Muslim, thought the committee was meant to harass Muslims at the university. When we started interviewing people to get their views on religious discord at the university, the very first interviewee said members of the committee could not be neutral because they were either victims or perpetrators of religious intolerance. The assignment was therefore a non-starter right from the beginning. I reported to the Chairperson of the Workers Council that we were unable to carry out the assignment; he on his part referred the issue back to the Workers Council. We in the committee had suggested that maybe this task should be given to an independent committee composed of members from outside the university. The assumption was that the new committee would be more objective than the previous one. However, the Workers Council eventually decided to sweep the issue under the carpet, arguing that after all there was no religious discord at the university. I was part of the Workers Council, so I was part of this decision. Nevertheless, with hindsight I think we did not make the right decision. Even if there were no religious discord, at least an independent committee would have told us why the allegations and suspicions to the contrary were so rampant.

## An Education System in Crisis

My tenure as Principal at the University of Dodoma opened my eyes to the deteriorating quality of education in the country. The quality of students we received from secondary schools was definitely worse than I had seen at the University of Dar es Salaam over the years I had been there. Each year we received a worse crop of students than the previous one. Students were unable to communicate fluently either in English or Kiswahili. The problem was not only the language, but also the inability to think clearly, in whatever language. Students were also ignorant of basic general knowledge about the world and even about Tanzania. One day I was shocked to learn that a second year university student did not even know the name of the Vice President of Tanzania, something even a Grade 2 pupil would be expected to know. On another occasion, a finalist student whose major subject was Kiswahili wrote a letter in Kiswahili which was incoherent. This, of course, is not something that one may solve at university level. It is a symptom of a bigger, more fundamental problem of the whole educational system in the country. Nor was this a problem faced by the University of Dodoma alone. My role as external examiner in Tanzania revealed the same problem in other universities as well.

These students seem to constitute a different generation, not really interested in the rigours of the academic life. Most students of the current generation would be happy to use shortcuts in order to get their certificates. This approach includes bribing their way up the educational ladder from primary school all the way to university level. Unfortunately, some parents and teachers are part of this dirty game, which explains why we have so many cases of forged certificates at all levels. We also have cases of students who pay people to write their dissertations for them. All these are worrying symptoms of a system that does not work properly. Unfortunately, these corrupt practices are not confined to students alone. We also have corruption even in the highest levels of government. There are very few people with the moral authority to condemn students involved in these malpractices.

Where will all this deterioration lead us to? Whenever I visit Dar es Salaam nowadays and I see so many young people in the streets doing nothing, my heart bleeds. Have we forsaken them? Is there nothing the society can do to channel this force to useful purpose? This time bomb is likely to explode any time. These are people who have nothing to lose, and they can very easily be used by selfish politicians to achieve their ends. We have already witnessed this scenario when churches in Dar es Salaam were attacked recently by so called 'angry Muslims.' Some of these youths were not even Muslims. All they wanted was a chance to vent their anger on a society which has forgotten them, and an opportunity to steal whatever they could lay their hands on.

We will have, over the years, an army of graduates at all levels of the educational system with no knowledge or skills, which means they cannot be employed. Some of them will be employed through corrupt practices, or because of 'technical know-who' instead of technical know-how. This situation will fuel incompetence and further corruption in the whole fabric of the society; it is a vicious circle. We will have a crop of leaders who are only interested in amassing wealth by any means, fair or foul, because that will be the only thing they are capable of doing. It will be a Machiavellian society where the end justifies the means.

Somebody said that in Africa people consume what they don't produce and produce what they don't consume. This system seems to be part of the reason why we don't make much progress. Certainly ostentatious consumption seems to be a malaise of many countries in Africa, both at individual and government level. Government spending is far beyond the means of the country. Top government officials are chauffeur-driven in very expensive four wheel drive vehicles. They pay themselves a lot of allowances, many of which cannot be justified in any way. The same officials own 'private' property, the grandeur of which is inconceivable in a poor country. Much of this 'private' property is in fact obtained by stealing public funds. One day I was amazed to see the Ambassador of Japan accredited to Tanzania being driven in a Toyota RAV4, a relatively cheap Japanese car. Yet Japan is the third biggest economy in the world after the USA and China. Surely the Japanese government can afford a more expensive car for their ambassador. I cannot, however, imagine an African ambassador being driven in a Toyota RAV4. When the Japanese Ambassador goes to sign documents for assisting Tanzania, he meets a government official who is being driven in a much more expensive Japanese car!

Sometimes I ask myself: why would one want to own ten cars? You can only drive one at a time. Why would one want to own ten mansions? You can only sleep in one room at a time, usually in a corner. You can only eat one meal at a time. While it is legitimate to seek to be comfortable in life by earning an honest income, living ostentatiously because of ill-gotten wealth is unacceptable. In any case, excessive wealth surrounded by misery is useless. You cannot enjoy this wealth, especially when you know quite well that people around you are miserable because you have stolen from them. Your conscience, assuming you have one, will always nag you.

Some people would, of course, say that this can be explained in terms of Maslow's hierarchy of needs. Human beings do not only need the basic necessities of life; they also want to excel. For some, amassing wealth is part of excelling; standing out from the rest of the crowd. This may be true, but my point is: you don't excel at the detriment of others; especially when the means you use are illegitimate. Moreover, in the developed countries and in the emerging economies of Asia, individuals excel by engaging in production of goods and services. In Africa, in most cases, people who are said to have made it in life are those engaged in conspicuous consumption without producing anything of value.

## Go, Sell Bread in your Country

When I first went to England for my M.A. studies, my wife asked me to bring her a sewing machine because she wanted to get involved in some small scale business. I obliged, and she immediately started making ladies' dresses. From 1983 to 2008 she was doing this business and expanded her business to not only making dresses, but also making tie and dye cloth. She increased the number of sewing machines from one in 1983 to 4 by 2008. Admittedly this is slow growth, but growth all the same. She had a steady, albeit small income. When we arrived in Dodoma, the number of clients went down because of the smaller size of Dodoma town. She was, therefore, getting less income than she had been getting in Dar es Salaam. All of a sudden, she said she wanted to change her line of business and start a bakery. At first I thought she was crazy, but eventually she managed to convince me that she was serious; that all she needed from me was some start-up capital and she would do the rest. I borrowed some money from the bank and she bought some equipment, rented premises, and started the bakery. To be frank, I thought I was making a big gamble with this money, but I was willing to take that risk to give her an opportunity to do what she wanted to do.

I was amazed by the outcome of this venture into the baking business. Within less than a year, my wife had managed to expand her business by buying more equipment and a van to distribute bread to different clients within Dodoma town. Her monthly net profit was already more than my salary as a professor. She had, within the first year, created employment for twelve people. Within three years, she had managed to move from the rented premises to her own building through a bank loan. She had also created more than thirty jobs.

What impresses me the most about my wife is her motivation to succeed against all odds. I admire her hard work, her focus on an idea and her sheer determination to see it through. It is my hope that my children will learn from their mother and have the courage and the determination to succeed in whatever they are doing.

At her work place, my wife is sometimes harassed by some customers. This takes the form of innuendos about foreigners who have come to take jobs which would otherwise belong to Tanzanians. She explains to them that she is a Tanzanian, even though she was born in Rwanda. She also tells them that she has not prevented anyone from doing what she is doing or any other business; and even if she closed her business this would not profit anyone of those complaining. More importantly, she reminds them that she is contributing to the growth of the economy, albeit in a small way, by creating jobs. They don't seem to be convinced. They simply do not accept her as a 'true' Tanzanian.

One of the employees at my wife's bakery was a woman who had come to ask for a job because she had problems with her husband. He did not provide for the family. My wife hired this woman, who was so grateful that she used to say that the bakery was her 'husband' and she couldn't imagine anything that would make her leave her employment because she had nowhere else to go. But as days went by, she started being arrogant and could not accept any reprimand when she did something wrong. One day, she dropped a bombshell. My son, who was at that time supervising work in the bakery, asked her why the place she was supposed to clean was still dirty. She said *"Hamkuja hapa kutunyanyasa sisi Watanzania. Rudini kwenu mkauze mikate huko"* (You didn't come here to harass us Tanzanians; go, sell bread in your country). My wife was shocked when she heard this. She confronted her and asked her where she would be without that employment. The woman apologized profusely; my wife forgave her and she continued working. A few weeks later, she said more or less the same thing, maybe thinking that again nothing would happen. This time it was too much for my wife, and she was sacked.

I have narrated this incident in some detail because it indicates the kind of attitude towards us as naturalized citizens of Tanzania; the fact that to many people we are still not really 'true' Tanzanians. I guess this perception is something that we have to live with. My wife and I have lived in Tanzania since the early 1960s. We have been citizens of Tanzania since 1980. Both of us are proficient in Kiswahili. Some of the people who question the citizenship of my wife were not yet born in 1980. The only thing that 'betrays' us are our physical features. To give an example, recently I checked into a hotel in Dar es Salaam. The receptionist asked me, "Are you a Tanzanian or a refugee?" I asked her, "Does it mean that if you are not a Tanzanian, then you are a refugee?" She was embarrassed and said I looked like a Somali or an Ethiopian. I told her I am a Tanzanian, and counselled her that she should never ask such questions to her hotel guests. I told her there was no nation or ethnic group of refugees. Anybody could be a refugee, including 'true' Tanzanians.

## Which Way Forward for Rwanda?

While at the University of Dodoma, I made several trips to Rwanda, some on official academic business and others privately to visit relatives and friends. On these trips I have seen changes that are happening in Rwanda since the genocide. The first thing that strikes a visitor to Rwanda is how clean the country is. This cleanliness is not only found in Kigali, the capital city, but throughout the whole country, whether you are in town or in the countryside. This perception, I must say, is not my biased assessment. Anybody who visits Rwanda has the same story: cleanliness, law and order, very little corruption.

There are very few African countries today for which you can say the same thing. The question is, why, of all the countries, is Rwanda succeeding where others have failed? Some people say that Rwanda is, and has always been, a land of law abiding citizens. This is both a strength and a weakness. Over the years, before, during and after colonialism, people of Rwanda have obeyed their leaders: the King, the catholic priests, the leadership after independence. That is why, it is argued, genocide happened in Rwanda. The leader tells you to go and kill your neighbour, you do it. If one follows this logic, one can explain why there is law and order in Rwanda today. However, this argument is rather simplistic and in some way insults the intelligence of Rwandese people. They are not robots that just follow orders. They know what is good for them, and certainly the history of Rwanda is so complex that it would be naive to reduce it to just obedience.

Some cynics say Rwanda is where it is today because Paul Kagame, the President of Rwanda, is a dictator. If he is and this is the secret behind the success story, maybe in Africa we need more dictators, not fewer.

I think there are two types of dictators: benevolent and malevolent. If Kagame is indeed a dictator, he is the former type and I see no problem with that because his 'dictatorship' is for the benefit of his countrymen and women. I think the reason he is called a dictator is because he is strict; he wants laws and regulations to be enforced. He pushes both himself and people around him to the limit to work hard. He also deals with defaulters without mercy. One Western observer of the Rwandese scene put it succinctly:

"In other countries, even the most successful people will do anything to become a minister. It means you can have a big car, a big house. People will bow before you, and you have a thousand ways to make yourself rich. Here it's just the opposite. It's not just that you have a low salary and no benefits of office. It's that when you work for Kagame, you are working 24 hours a day. The ministers absolutely dread those Wednesday afternoon cabinet meetings. Kagame is so sharp with them. He will look right at a minister and say, "I'm not satisfied. You are not performing well. Either improve or I will find someone else" (Kinzer p.237-238).

On one of my recent visits, I had an opportunity to visit a district office in the west of the country. On the door of each office, there is a photograph of the person in charge of the office and his/her mobile telephone number. There is also the telephone number of the immediate boss. I was told this display was meant to ensure every customer gets the service they deserve without undue bureaucratic red tape. If one is not satisfied, they have the right to complain to the person next in hierarchy. I was also told that each officer has a set of targets that have to be reached by the end of the financial year. If those targets have not been met, the officer has to give a convincing explanation; otherwise they have to take responsibility, including being dismissed. This, I was told, is at all levels of government.

One, of course, hears some commentators, especially those from the West, say that what is happening in Rwanda is not typically African. As if Africa is expected and meant to be perpetually mediocre. If other continents can have progress and put in place functioning systems, why not Africa? I think that is what Kagame is trying to show to the world. I am not suggesting that President Kagame is perfect. I guess he would be the last person to claim that himself. As a human being he does make mistakes, especially given the very difficult environment (because of Rwanda's history) his government is working in. He also has political enemies, both Hutu and Tutsi, who will do everything in their power to try and derail him from his vision of a prosperous Rwanda, or who might even have legitimate concerns about his leadership. I am not an apologist for Kagame. What is said here is not in any way a comment on errors President Kagame might have made, or any crimes he is often alleged to have committed. These alleged crimes have never, to the best of my knowledge, been proved in any court of law. All I am saying is, whatever shortcomings Kagame might have as a leader – Don't we all as human beings have shortcomings? – he has tried his best to move Rwanda from the gates of hell in 1994 to the next level of socio-economic development.

In many other African countries – there are of course exceptions to the rule – one gets the impression that nothing works. Public transport is inefficient, so everybody wants to buy a car. Many cars on narrow roads make traffic jams intolerable. The sewage system is always clogged. We blame the municipal authorities for doing nothing about it, but as we complain, we throw garbage in the very sewer that is already clogged. The national airline is a joke. Our leaders fly in other people's airlines and shower them with praise. The railway system does not work because some very influential people in government would lose their business in road haulage if the railway system were efficient. As a result, the roads are overwhelmed by heavy trucks and cannot last for a long time; that is assuming they were not sub-standard in the first place. We disregard the law and build wherever there is space, even if that space is on the road reserve. When our houses are demolished, we complain to the government and say we are citizens and therefore no one should touch us, even if we defecate in front of our neighbour's house. We complain about corruption, yet we are the first to want shortcuts by giving 'something small' for a service which we have the right to get. We forget that shortcuts are almost always wrong cuts. In brief, people complain that things are not right in their country, but most of them do nothing to make things work. In fact they act in such a way that makes things worse. We forfeit our responsibility to make the system work, blaming the 'government' for everything as if we are not part of the government. We want change, but we do nothing to bring about that change.

What we see in many African countries is that politicians are more concerned with the immediate, instead of the important. Thus, for example, it is more likely politicians will ensure more schools are built, without necessarily thinking about facilities or training teachers. Buildings are easier to show to the electorate in order to win votes. So, quantity becomes more important than quality.

Having painted a positive picture of Rwanda after the genocide, I must also say the other impression one gets on visiting the country is that despite the impressive progress made since the genocide, there are still undercurrents of mistrust between the Hutu and the Tutsi. People don't say it openly, but, in private conversations with close friends, it is clear that the two sides don't trust each other. What will it take for the two ethnic groups to trust each other? This is a difficult question; I cannot pretend that I have an easy answer for it. I, however, think that the first step towards reconciliation is not to poison the minds of the young generation with old prejudices and stereotypes. Given what has happened, this is not easy either, but doing nothing is not an option. Political will on the part of leaders is essential; so is civic education. People have to know the truth about what has been going on in Rwanda for centuries, but they also need to make an effort to give true reconciliation a chance.

A Rwandese artist has recently composed a song with words which best capture what needs to be done in the aftermath of the genocide in Rwanda. He says, among other things: *umujinya mwiza si umurandura nzuzi; umwanzi wa mbere n'ubujiji n'ubukene* (Positive anger does not uproot seeds; and the main enemies are ignorance and poverty). In other words, the Rwandese people are justified to be angry at what happened to them, but their anger should not be destructive. Instead, they should change it into positive energy to fight ignorance and poverty. At the end of the day, if these two enemies are not confronted, they engender a time bomb that may lead to another cataclysm. True reconciliation can only come when people have got rid of their ignorance and poverty.

Sometimes people draw parallels between the Tutsi and the Jews. For one thing, both groups have experienced a threat of extermination: the Jews under the German Nazis during World War II, and the Tutsi during the 1959 'Hutu revolution' and, especially, the 1994 genocide. Maybe because of this threat of extermination, both groups are preoccupied with survival strategies, which could unfortunately verge on paranoia if not properly managed. Their past histories may have led them to be too aggressive in pursuit of self-preservation. However, while the Jews have a big brother, the United States of America, to protect them, the Tutsi have none. In fact, they are mistrusted by all the neighbouring countries; they are suspected of being expansionist with dreams of establishing a 'Hima empire' in East and Central Africa. This mistrust is, to the best of my knowledge, not founded on any tangible evidence.

Rwanda has a chance of building a stable, prosperous nation under the current leadership. However, my view is that stability and prosperity in Rwanda will depend on whether people are prepared to work together towards that end. We know that there are people both inside and outside the country who, for their own selfish interests, are prepared to undermine the efforts of the majority of the people of Rwanda in bringing about their development. This has nothing to do with being Hutu or Tutsi. The opponents of the current government come from the two sides, Hutu and Tutsi. Of course individuals with political ambition will always exploit the historical mistrust between the two groups for their own ends.

## An Education Through Travel

There is a Kinyarwanda proverb that goes: *akanyoni katagurutse ntikamenya aho bweze* (a bird that does not fly cannot know where there is abundant food). Travelling has taught me quite a lot of things, so metaphorically I got a lot of food for thought from my different travels abroad. I have, over the years, visited the following countries: Botswana, Burundi, Ethiopia, Ghana, Kenya, Malawi, Mali, Mauritius, Mozambique, South Africa, Swaziland, Uganda (Africa); Belgium, France, Germany, Italy, Norway, Spain, Sweden, Switzerland, United Kingdom (Europe); China, India (Asia); United Arab Emirates (Middle East).

The first thing I learnt from my different trips abroad is that there is no superior or inferior culture. Cultures are simply different. When one travels, one feels cultural shock at first, but afterwards one gets used to what at first had seemed strange. I have mentioned earlier that during my first visit to England, I was shocked that people don't talk to each other on trains or buses. Years later when I visited West Africa, I was equally shocked that people 'shouted' when talking to each other. Even within East Africa, there are remarkable differences. In Kenya, when you go to a bar, you literally order the bar tender to serve you: *"lete bia"* (bring me a bottle of beer). In Tanzania, that would be extremely rude; you would say: *"tafadhali naomba bia"* (could you please give me a bottle of beer). So, people's behaviour is relative and what one sees as normal, another person might see as abnormal behaviour. It all depends on your yardstick.

The second lesson I learnt from my travels, especially outside Africa, is that people take their jobs seriously. In the countries I have visited in Europe and in Asia, people don't give lame excuses for being absent from their job. In contrast, in Africa there are always a thousand and one reasons for not coming to work: a sick relative (and a very distant one for that matter), the funeral of the friend of a former neighbour, prayers for the departed uncle in the spouse's clan, the list is long. If you are the boss in a workplace and refuse permission, everybody is up in arms and you are accused of harassing the employees.

Although I had already travelled overseas widely before going to the University of Dodoma, two trips abroad while at the University of Dodoma have probably made the most lasting impression on me. In 2010, I travelled to India for a medical check-up and treatment. I had been referred to Apollo Hospital in Bangalore, southern India. India is one of the fastest growing economies in the world. It is today part of what is called the emerging economies, and part of the BRICS (Brazil, Russia, India, China, South Africa) block. India has made big strides in the ICT industry, so much so that Bangalore is now called the Silicon Valley of Asia. In the medical field, the Apollo hospitals in India (New Delhi, Chennai, Bangalore, Hyderabad) are well known throughout the world for their cutting edge health delivery services. While in Bangalore, I met patients from different corners of the world who had come for medical attention. Today, Americans and Europeans go to India for what is called medical tourism. They get first class treatment for a fraction of what they would have paid for such treatment at home.

I had been referred to India by a consultant cardiologist in Dar es Salaam. I had been on treatment for several months, but my doctor wanted me to undergo some medical tests which could not be done in Tanzania. When I arrived at the Apollo Hospital in Bangalore, I was admitted and some routine tests were made before the main test I had come for. When the test was finally done, it took 20 minutes. So I had to come all the way to India, with all associated costs, for a test that took only 20 minutes. I started asking myself if it would not have been much cheaper if the facilities had been in Tanzania. Certainly I was not the only person to go to India for medical treatment. Many people are sent by the government almost on a daily basis. If the government were to put resources into referral hospitals in the country, this would no doubt make it much cheaper, and much more convenient to be treated within Tanzania.

India is doing very well economically, but it is still a poor country. There are millions of people who still live in abject poverty. The benefits of economic growth have not yet trickled down to the ordinary citizens. Part of this delay, it is often claimed in different quarters of the world, is because of rampant corruption in the country. I personally experienced this while in Bangalore, although I cannot generalize from just one incident, especially given that I stayed in India for only one week. In India you have to report to the police within seven days of arriving in the country for your passport to be endorsed. When I arrived at the Apollo Hospital, my son who had accompanied me went to the nearest police station to have our passports endorsed. The first day he was not successful; he was told to go back the following day. He went to the police station every day for the six days I was admitted in the hospital, and we were anxious because we were about to leave, and the seven-day deadline was approaching. On the sixth day, an employee of the hospital went with him. He talked to the police officer on duty in the local language and 'greased his hand' with some rupees. The passports were immediately endorsed.

I travelled to China in 2012 as part of a delegation from the University of Dodoma, which went to finalize the process of establishing a Confucius Institute at the University of Dodoma. We were led by our Vice-Chancellor, Prof. Idris Kikula. The other member of the delegation was Prof. Ludovick Kinabo, Deputy Vice-Chancellor (Academic, Research and Consultancy). We spent only six days in China, but during this short visit I was very impressed by the progress China has made in just over 60 years since the Communist Party came to power in 1949 under Chairman Mao Zedong. From a very poor agrarian society, China is now the second biggest economy in the world, after the USA. The secret behind this spectacular success is hard work.

I was also impressed by the rich cultural heritage which goes back several millennia. A visit to the Great Wall was breath-taking; I had never seen anything like that in my life. No doubt it is one of the wonders of the world; and the Chinese have a saying that you are not a hero until you have climbed the Great Wall. I did climb the Great Wall, but the first stage was to go into a cable car in order to reach the wall itself. I must confess that the cable car experience was a bit frightening. When you look down into the valley over which the car is travelling, you just wonder what would happen if the cables were to snap suddenly. The answer is clear, definitely it is death. We were assured during the briefing that the cable cars are safe, but that does not prevent one from engaging in flights of imagination.

The Forbidden City gives you a feel of the splendour of life lived by ancient Chinese Emperors. A more recent revolutionary 'emperor',

Chairman Mao Zedong, can still be seen in his mausoleum near Tiananmen Square. One would think he is just lying there, asleep. The visit to Shaolin Temple in Henan Province near the city of Zhengzhou, and especially the cultural show that we attended one evening, was surreal. It was like I was just drifting in a beautiful dream which I didn't want to end.

But the visit to China also left me with unanswered questions. Why is it that the Chinese are interested in establishing Confucius Institutes all over the world? Is it really a project without any hidden agenda? Could this be a new type of linguistic imperialism in competition with English linguistic imperialism? Robert Phillipson thinks that the spread of English in the world is to a large extent due to the imperial expansion of both England and the United States of America, and that the dominance of English in the world today serves the interests of global capitalism led by the United States of America. Certainly one would expect the quest for resources and investment opportunities that China is now involved in would go hand in hand with influencing people's world view in different parts of the world. The spread of the Chinese language through the establishment of Confucius Institutes is, in my view, part of this global Chinese strategy. We are already witnessing Chinese companies in Tanzania, as well as in other African countries, involved in big construction projects (roads, railways, big government and corporate buildings), as well as in wholesale and retail trade. It would be naïve to think that the cultural influence sought through the establishment of Confucius Institutes is detached from this economic onslaught.

I also realized, while in China, that the great economic strides made were at the expense of the environment. Air pollution in Beijing (and in other Chinese cities) is a very serious concern. It is common to see cyclists and pedestrians wearing face masks as a precaution against inhaling polluted air. Of course environmental degradation is not only a Chinese problem. It is a problem throughout the world, especially the industrialized countries of the West. However, while the USA and Western Europe have their fair share of environmental pollution, they are always up in arms, blaming China for doing exactly what they did in order to arrive at the economic development they presently enjoy. I think the lesson we can learn here is that environmental degradation is a global challenge that calls for a global strategy to confront it. Blaming each other is not going to solve the problem.

## End of Contract at the University of Dodoma

When I first came to Dodoma in 2008, I signed a four year contract which ended in September 2012. I asked for renewal of the contract, but the process of getting approval from the President's office (Public Service, or as popularly known, *Utumishi*) took a long time. I continued working, while waiting for the approval to come through. This time I was being paid from the university's own sources of income, having been removed from the government payroll. The first decision of *Utumishi* was negative. My contract could not be renewed because I was over 65, and a new circular from *Utumishi* had just been out, to the effect that no one above 65 would get contract employment in a public institution. Apparently the university management appealed on my behalf, arguing that I still had an important role to play, especially mentoring young academic members of staff who would eventually take over from me. The response from *Utumishi* on this appeal again took some time. When it eventually came in the middle of June 2013, it was still negative. I had to leave University of Dodoma employment. I had reached my "sell by" date!

Meanwhile, around the same time, academic staff in the College of Humanities and Social Sciences were threatening to go on strike because they had not been paid their invigilation and marking allowances. We had told them that the college did not have any money to pay them at that time; that they should be patient until funds are disbursed. They did not want to listen; they wanted their money immediately, otherwise they would go on strike, which would disrupt the end of year examinations. Unfortunately, somebody in the university central administration sided with the lecturers, agreeing with them that the college was wrong not to pay them. However, this person knew quite well that the college, indeed the whole university, did not have any money to pay the lecturers' allowances. The refusal of *Utumishi* to extend my contract was then hijacked and it was handled in such a way as to be interpreted as my being removed because of incompetence. Indeed, the leaders of UDOMASA, who had been in the forefront, fighting for the "right" to be paid immediately, celebrated their "victory" over me when they heard I was leaving.

The whole process of my departure was deliberately intended to placate UDOMASA at my expense. On 11th June 2013, I was called to the central administration and told verbally that *Utumishi* had not approved the extension of my contract. Almost immediately the same day a press release was out, and an acting principal was appointed even before I had been given a letter to revoke my appointment as principal. At the same time, the Chief Internal Auditor was instructed to audit the accounts of the college. Of course the message being sent was that the central administration suspected there might be some misuse of the college funds. I learnt later that even the Chancellor, who was the appointing authority of principals, was not consulted about my removal, nor was the Chairman of the University Council. I was shocked. How could an Acting Principal be appointed before I was formally told that I had to hand over my duties as Principal? On 14th June, I went to complain to the Vice-Chancellor about how this matter was being handled, and I was told it was an oversight. The same day a letter was written to me and brought to my house after 9.00 p.m. when I was about to retire to bed. The letter said my contract had been renewed for two years with effect from 1st July 2011 and that it was due to expire on 30th June 2013. This was not true. I had been appointed Principal for a second term of three years with effect from 1st July 2011, so my tenure was due to end on 30th June 2014. Nothing was said about this appointment, and it was never revoked by the relevant authority, i.e. the Chancellor of the University of Dodoma.

It was unfortunate that my stay at the University of Dodoma had to end like this. I had enjoyed my job both as a professor of linguistics and as a Principal. I saw the university (and the College of Humanities and Social Sciences) grow rapidly during the time I was there. It was both a satisfying and challenging journey. I am sure I made some contribution which called for a bit more respect than I got at the end of this sojourn. It really pained me that after five years of service, I would be treated like this. I feel I was treated like a piece of sugar cane: You chew it, swallow the sweet juice and spit out the useless residue. What exactly did I do to deserve this? Maybe I will never know the real truth behind this saga. It is possible that even before the lecturers' allowances issue there was something else going on that I did not know. Whatever the truth may be, I can only say I wish the University of Dodoma was run in a better way than it is at the moment. This is not crying foul because I am no longer there. I have the greatest admiration and respect for the majority of the people in the administration of the university. But some few people are making it difficult for the university to run smoothly because they want cheap popularity. The politics of appeasement have never worked anywhere.

Two months after my leaving the University of Dodoma, I got a "thank you note" from the Vice-Chancellor, expressing gratitude for the contribution I had made to the university. Reading between the lines, I had the impression that the letter was written grudgingly, maybe after pressure from some colleagues, otherwise why did it take two months to decide to write? I responded to the note in a respectful manner, but really in my heart of hearts I thought this was too little too late.

Even after leaving the University of Dodoma, I continued supervising my M.A. and Ph.D. students. I did not see any reason for punishing them for the mistreatment I got from the university administration.

Despite this treatment, my five years as Principal of the College of Humanities and Social Sciences at the University of Dodoma was time I will always remember and cherish. It built my capacity both as an academic and as a leader. My M.A. classes over the five years, as well as several Ph.D. students I supervised to successful completion, were very rewarding. I will always remember the heated debates I had with my students on the role of language in education in Tanzania in particular, and in Africa more generally.

My stay at the University of Dodoma also opened my eyes to the challenges of a new university in Tanzania. These included, but were not limited to, challenges of cash flow, inexperienced academic leadership especially at departmental level, young academics who are more interested in money than in building a solid academic career and weak management. Leaders at university and college levels were sometimes at loggerheads as to the best way of managing the university. Decentralisation was especially a very charged topic. While top management were rather reluctant to allow decentralisation, College Principals thought some kind of decentralisation was necessary for the efficient running of a big institution like the University of Dodoma. I remember one day the Chairman of the University Council warned both sides about their rigid positions on the issue of decentralisation. He said a lot of centralisation is like constipation; the system gets clogged and nothing moves. On the other hand, decentralisation without control is like diarrhoea; the system is let loose. There was need, therefore, for striking a balance between the two.

Beijing, China (30th May 2012): The Vice-Chancellor of the University of Dodoma, Prof. Idris Kikula (front left), exchanging the instruments for the establishment of the Confucius Institute at the University of Dodoma with the CEO of the Confucius Institute (Headquarters), Ms. Xu Lin (front right). Prof. Ludovick Kinabo (centre) and Prof. Casmir Rubagumya (back left) are looking on.

Chapter Six

# St. John's University of Tanzania

When I completed my contract at the University of Dodoma, I decided to apply for a teaching post at St. John's University of Tanzania, whose main campus is in Dodoma. I had no intention of going back to Dar es Salaam, and I still felt strong enough to continue working. I certainly could not see myself staying at home doing nothing.

So, for the first time in my life, I wrote a letter of application for a job. Hitherto, I had always been offered jobs without having to formally apply. I waited for about a week, then one afternoon somebody who identified himself as a member of staff from St. John's University called me on my mobile phone. He wanted to confirm if I had applied for a job at his university, and I said yes, I had indeed. He then asked me if I could come to the university that afternoon for what he called some consultation. I said, no problem I would come. We agreed to meet at 3:00pm. When I arrived at the administration block, he was there waiting for me. He took me to his office and left me for about 10 minutes.

When he came back, he told me I was going for an interview for the post of Deputy Vice-Chancellor (Academics). This announcement took me by surprise on two counts. First, he had not told me in advance that I was being called for an interview. Second, I had applied for a teaching post, not an administrative one. Be that as it may, I was taken into a room where a panel of eight people was waiting to interview me. The interview was conducted in a very relaxed manner and after about 45 minutes it was over.

I was told I would be contacted in due course. As it turned out, I had to wait for slightly more than two months to get some feedback. Eventually, on 9ᵗʰ September 2013, I got a letter of appointment to the post of Deputy Vice-Chancellor (Academics) from the Chancellor, Archbishop (Rtd) Donald Leo Mtetemela. The tenure was for a term of four years.

## The Fragility of Legal Citizenship

During the intervening two months between leaving the University of Dodoma and joining St. John's University of Tanzania, relations between Tanzania and Rwanda were rather tense. Illegal immigrants into Tanzania from Rwanda and other neighbouring countries were being expelled from Tanzania. This action in itself was nothing unusual: a country should ensure that people who enter its borders do so legally. Unfortunately, the expulsion coincided with a diplomatic row between Rwanda and Tanzania and a war of words between leaders of the two countries, fuelled by the media. Although my family and I had nothing to fear because we are legally staying in Tanzania as naturalized citizens, we were all the same a bit anxious because we were hearing stories of people of Rwandese origin whose naturalization certificates were being torn by village leaders and owners ordered to leave the country. This was especially so in rural areas in Kagera Region. I have no evidence to confirm these stories, but naturally they made us extremely insecure.

All these happenings made me reflect on the fragility of citizenship by naturalisation. Are such citizens protected by the law like citizens by birth? If indeed it is true that some people in Karagwe had their naturalisation certificates torn by local leaders, what recourse in law did they have? Did anybody stand up on their behalf to protest this illegal action?

## Learning to Manage a Private University

The day I reported to St. John's University to take up my post as Deputy Vice-Chancellor (Academics), I met the Vice-Chancellor, Prof. Gabriel Mwaluko. He introduced me to the person who had been Acting Deputy Vice-Chancellor (Academics), Prof. Mombo Kamwaya. Prof. Kamwaya was, paradoxically, the person to whom I had submitted my application letter for a teaching position. That day there was a management meeting in the morning and I was introduced to deans and directors. The Vice-Chancellor chaired only part of the meeting because he had to leave for Dar es Salaam for a medical check-up. As it turned out, that was my first and last time to see Prof. Mwaluko. He stayed in Dar es Salaam for a few days, and then he was referred to India for treatment. He stayed in India for about two months. On 19th November 2013, he died at the Apollo Hospital, Hyderabad. He was buried on 23rd November 2013 in his home village Chikuyu, in Manyoni District, Singida Region.

Prof. Mwaluko's death was a shock to the whole university community and to me personally. While he was away in India, he had left two senior academic staff, Dr. Assad Kipanga and Dr. John Ham, to act on his behalf. Normally, the Deputy Vice-Chancellor (Academics) would have been left in the acting position in accordance with the university charter. However, since I had just joined the university, it was understood that in all fairness to me, I should be given a bit of time to familiarize myself with the new environment. In any case, we all thought that this arrangement would be just for a short time and that the Vice-Chancellor would be back very soon.

On 26th November 2013, the Chancellor, Archbishop (Rtd) Donald Mtetemela, in consultation with the Chairman of the University Council, appointed me Acting Vice-Chancellor. I accepted the appointment with trepidation. I had been at the university for hardly three months. Although at the University of Dodoma I had headed a college with more students than the whole of St. John's University, I still felt that heading a university, especially when still new to the place, was going to be difficult. Moreover, for the whole of my career as a university don, I had hitherto worked in public universities. This was a private university under the Anglican Church of Tanzania. The ethos was bound to be different. In addition to that, as a Catholic I realized that my religious beliefs and practices might not always be in line with what was expected of the top leader of an Anglican establishment. I, therefore, knew that I had a lot to learn about the culture and the politics of this new institution. The situation I found myself in reminded me of a prayer by an American theologian, Reinhold Neibuhr:

God, grant me the serenity
to accept the things I cannot change,
the courage to change the things I can,
and the wisdom to know the difference.

In this new position, I really needed the serenity, the courage and the wisdom to be able to discharge my responsibilities.

My first test came just a few weeks after assuming the position of Acting Vice-Chancellor. Certificate and diploma students doing programmes in laboratory technology almost went on strike, demanding to do medical laboratory technology instead of general laboratory technology. I came to learn that this problem had started the previous year, and somehow it had been allowed to continue without being sorted out. I was now under intense pressure both from students and their parents to resolve this problem. I started getting phone calls from parents enquiring about the fate of their children. Some asked politely; others spoke with veiled threats about the consequences of not resolving the problem to their satisfaction. I and my colleagues had to weather that storm as diplomatically as we could. We eventually managed to get the programmes registered and recognized by both the Ministry of Health and the National Council for Technical Education (NACTE).

My first priority as Acting Vice-Chancellor was to ensure there was an active organizational structure. I had noted that some of the committees, for example, were dormant. I had to revive them. I had also to streamline some of the committees that were rather big in terms of membership. This, in my view, was a recipe for inefficiency and ineffectiveness. Furthermore, I wanted to ensure that strategic ideas left behind by the late Prof. Mwaluko were carefully considered and implemented. That was the least we could do to keep his spirit alive among us. One of these strategic ideas was to establish a teaching centre at Kigoma for running certificate and diploma programmes in business studies and community work.

My other priority was to instil discipline in whatever we were doing as a university. For example, when I took over as Deputy Vice-Chancellor (Academics) I was told by colleagues that transcripts and certificates were always late. In fact, people who had graduated the previous year were still coming to enquire about their certificates, one year later. I pushed the examinations office and the data base team, and during the 2013 graduation ceremony we were able to announce to the graduating students that their certificates were ready.

Financial discipline was another area of concern. Financial transactions were made without adequate internal controls. As Acting Vice-Chancellor, I worked with the newly appointed Chief Internal Auditor to enforce financial regulations.

At a retreat of deans, directors and other senior managers of the university that was held shortly after my appointment as Acting Vice-Chancellor, I underscored to my colleagues the importance of working together as a team: We need to row in the same direction, I told them; We need to have one chain of command with a clear demarcation of who does what; We should not look the other way when somebody needs to be disciplined; Leaders have to make the right decisions even when those decisions are not pleasant to everybody. I also emphasized that we should uphold the principle of collective responsibility as university managers.

The issue of our identity as a Christian university and the university's motto "to learn to serve" came to the fore of our discussions. What does it mean to be a Christian university? Is it enough to start and end our meetings with a prayer and to have a crucifix hanging on the wall in the Council Chamber? We needed to go beyond these external tokens and do some soul searching. We needed to ask ourselves whether we were really committed to learning in order to serve our students, the community surrounding us and the nation, for that is the real spirit of a Christian ethos.

I challenged my colleagues to stop complaining about inadequate resources and do something to mobilize more resources for their respective units. I put it to them that lack of resources is not the only challenge that can derail our vision and mission. Intrigues, rumour mongering, corruption, indiscipline and poor management were all serious challenges to the well-being of our university.

Some of the challenges I encountered at St. John's had to do with uncooperative staff. This was especially so with academic staff in the School of Pharmacy and the Faculty of Natural Sciences. In the School of Pharmacy, three senior academic members of staff spent most of their time doing personal consultancies, which they never reported to the university as per the consultancy policy. They compressed their teaching within a very short period of time, thus inconveniencing students. The justification they gave for this schedule was that they had agreed with the Vice-Chancellor, Prof. Mwaluko, that they would be allowed flexibility in their teaching schedules in order to accommodate their consultancies. However, this 'agreement' was not documented anywhere. We in management tried to show them it would be difficult to have two sets of treatment for academic staff. After a long tug of war, we eventually agreed that they would surrender 30% of their monthly salary in return for being allowed to take 30% of university time to do their consultancies. I was surprised that after a few days of this agreement, one of them came to me and said even this was not acceptable. He wanted to take leave without pay. Obviously he had not come to the negotiating table in good faith.

In the Faculty of Natural Sciences, the biggest problem was lack of leadership. The Dean and the Associate Dean (Academic) were really not on top of what was going on in the faculty. They would make wrong decisions or give wrong information to different decision- making organs. When taken to task, the dean would be very aggressive as a defensive mechanism, never accepting wrong doing. The medical laboratory technology crisis mentioned above was created by both wrong action and inaction by the Faculty of Natural Sciences leadership.

In dealing with administrative staff, one incident I vividly remember was a showdown with one Admissions Officer, Mr. Karshia. Many people had been complaining about the behaviour of this young man. He was always arrogant, disrespectful and was in office when he wanted. One day I called him to my office. When I summoned him, he was not in office. He had left without any permission. He came some 30 minutes after I had sent for him. When I asked him why he had gone out of office without permission, he had no acceptable answer. When I asked him why he was always rude to customers, he said arrogantly that there was no evidence of those allegations. I asked him why he was not signing the attendance register like everybody else, he had no answer. His whole attitude and demeanour in my office was of a person with no respect to authority and no remorse for what he was doing. I told him he had to change, or, if he thought St. John's was not good enough for him, he should leave. There were no sacred cows at the university, I told him in no uncertain terms; either he complied with the rules and regulations and behaved properly or he left. A few days later he tendered his resignation. When I heard this I said to myself, good riddance!

Dodoma, Tanzania (4th December 2013): The author delivering a speech at the fourth graduation ceremony of St. John's University of Tanzania, in his capacity as Acting Vice-Chancellor.

On 3rd July 2014, the Board of Trustees of St. John's University (House of Bishops of the Anglican Church of Tanzania) endorsed the council recommendation for the appointment of Reverend Prof. Emmanuel Mbennah as the new Vice-Chancellor of St. John's University of Tanzania. One of the qualifications for the person to be appointed

Vice-Chancellor was that he had to be an Anglican. Although I had all the academic qualifications and leadership experience, I was not even short listed for an interview during the search process because I am not Anglican.

I did not feel any bitterness for not being considered for the job. In fact I had expected all along that this would be the case. It is good for the identity of the university as an Anglican institution to be led by an Anglican, this time with the added advantage that Prof. Mbennah is also an ordained Anglican priest. I was happy to work with the new Vice-Chancellor in my capacity as Deputy Vice-Chancellor (Academics). This appointment was indeed good news for me because it would lessen the burden of leading the university. However, the bad news was that Prof. Mbennah was not available immediately. He was working in South Africa, and he intimated that he could only report to take up his new position towards the end of the year. I, therefore, still had to soldier on as Acting Vice-Chancellor until he returned from South Africa. This time was particularly difficult for the university because of the unfavourable financial situation. For example, for July 2014 we had to borrow money from a bank in order to pay staff salaries. We just managed to pay net salary for August, and the September salary was not paid until mid-October.

Reverend Prof. Mbennah officially reported to take up his position on 22nd September 2014. He spent four days at the university, in his own words "seeing and listening". In other words, this was an opportunity for him to see the university, get introduced to staff and students, and listen to different people in order to understand what was going on. However, the new Vice-Chancellor did more than just "seeing and listening". He talked to management as well as to the whole university community, and his words were so uplifting. We were all impressed by his vision for the university and his spirit of optimism. By the end of his short stay, everybody was left with very high expectations. After the four days, he had to go back to South Africa to wind up his business with his employer. He was expected back on a more permanent basis in November. We couldn't wait for him to return!

When the Vice-Chancellor eventually came in November, he was unfortunately met by a student strike. Students must have planned this to coincide with his arrival in order to 'test the waters' and see how he would handle the situation. No sooner had the Vice-Chancellor started dealing with the student strike than academic members of staff also started what they called an 'extended meeting' to deliberate on their problems. For all intents and purposes, this was also a strike. Again, it would seem likely that this was also planned to coincide with the arrival of the Vice-Chancellor.

Both students and academic staff had a long list of grievances against the University administration, most of which were normal challenges facing any University, especially to do with limited resources. However, some were genuine concerns mainly to do with lack of accountability and transparency on the part of some university managers. The Vice-Chancellor promised to solve the problems that were in his capacity to solve within the shortest possible time. Overall, the Vice- Chancellor handled the crisis very well. This was his 'baptism of fire'!

He demonstrated to the students and staff that he was ready to listen, dialogue and try and solve genuine problems, but that he would not be pushed around!

My experience at St. John's University of Tanzania had some similarities with that at the University of Dodoma. First, both universities were relatively young, both having been established in 2007. Second, like the University of Dodoma, St. John's University also had the challenge of being run by young inexperienced academics, especially at departmental level. Third, there were very few academic members of staff at higher levels. Here also most academic staff were Tutorial Assistants and Assistant Lecturers.

However, there were also differences. To start with, St. John's University is a private Christian University while the University of Dodoma is public. This in itself is a big difference especially in terms of funding. While public universities get salaries of their employees from the government, private universities depend on tuition fees to pay salaries. Furthermore, being a Christian University, St. John's does not only focus on academic learning, it also puts emphasis on inculcating among staff and students a Christian ethos, enshrined in its motto "to learn to serve".

# Chapter Seven

# Conclusion

Earlier in this story, I said Rwanda gave me my heart and Tanzania gave me my brain and that it is difficult to choose between my heart and my brain. I should now say that it is not even necessary to choose between the two. My cultural heritage is heavily skewed towards Rwanda, while my intellectual growth has been greatly shaped by Tanzania. I therefore consider myself a son of two countries.

Anyone who comes to my home will see cultural artefacts from Rwanda: *uduseke* (traditional baskets), *ibyansi* (traditional wooden milk jugs) and pieces of *imigongo* (wall decorations from Gisaka, eastern Rwanda). I enjoy the Rwandese traditional dances, *guhamiriza* for men and *kubyina* for women. So, my cultural heritage is mainly Rwandese. I should, however, say that this does not mean Tanzania has not contributed anything to my cultural heritage. If culture is seen in its wider context as a way of life, then certainly Tanzania has contributed to my cultural heritage. Any Rwandese who has lived in Tanzania for a considerable length of time is always seen as behaving in a specific way which is typically Tanzanian. That is why the Rwandese who had been in Tanzania and went back to Rwanda after 1994 are called aba-TZ (returnees from Tanzania). This is not only a comment on the geographical location from where they came, it is mainly a comment on their behaviour. For example, unlike those who came from Uganda, Kenya, the Democratic Republic of Congo and Burundi, aba-TZ are well known for how they help each other during social occasions like funerals and wedding ceremonies. I should, therefore, say that I have a double cultural heritage.

Again, if language is part of culture – and I believe it is – then Tanzania has greatly contributed to my linguistic repertoire. This is why, for instance, I am writing this story in English, not in Kinyarwanda. I would have written it in Kiswahili, but I don't feel comfortable writing formal Kiswahili, having worked mainly in English for the whole of my professional life. In formal use of language, I certainly feel more comfortable writing in English, less in Kiswahili; even least in Kinyarwanda. As for my children, they understand Kinyarwanda, but cannot speak it fluently. For all intents and purposes, their mother-tongue is Kiswahili.

This is not to say that my heart is only in Rwanda. The fact that I have chosen to remain in Tanzania and to dedicate my whole career to educating Tanzanians, when I had an option of going back to Rwanda, would demonstrate that my heart belongs to both countries.

With regard to the brain, my intellectual growth has mainly been shaped by Tanzania for obvious reasons. Apart from the nearly seven years of primary education in Rwanda, my education and academic life has almost entirely been in Tanzania, with extended periods of stay in England for my graduate studies (both M.A. and Ph.D.).

However, even in this area, the picture is a little bit more complex. I think the one and a half years I spent at École Normale Zaza did contribute to my intellectual development and my philosophical outlook, even if the time was short and I was still an adolescent. For example, of all the songs we were taught by Frère Auxille, I still vividly remember one song, which has made a great impression on my mind, and which has guided my philosophical outlook over the years.

I reproduce it below with my English translation, although I may not do justice to the original poetic French.

*Un sentier serpente, parmi les buissons*
*Et sa forte pente, nous la connaissons*
*C'est la route pure, de l'idéal*
*Ou ne s'aventure jamais le mal*
*C'est la route dure, vers les hauteurs*
*C'est la route sure du vrai bonheur.*
*L'âme ne se lève, qu'au prix de l'effort*
*Et rien ne s'achève, sans souffrance et mort.*

## English translation

*A meandering path in the wilderness*
*And to its steep slopes we bear witness*
*It is a pure route of an ideal life*
*Where no evil dares to tread*
*It is a difficult route towards the summit*
It is a sure route of real happiness
*The soul cannot soar without making an effort*
*And nothing is achieved without suffering and death.*

For me, this song encapsulates my life journey. Most probably the song articulates the life journey of most other human beings like me. If I were to summarize this song in two phrases, I would simply say "nothing comes easy, and suffering and death are part of life on earth". This is my life story, and I hope my children and my grandchildren and anybody else who happens to read it will learn something from how I learned to love two countries and from how I embraced education at all stages of this life.

# Works Cited

Kinzer, Stephen (2008) A Thousand Hil s: Rwanda's Rebirth and the Man Who Dreamed It. New Jersey: John Wiley & Sons.

Mamdani, Mahmood (2001) When Victims Become Kil ers: Colonialism, Nativism and the Genocide in Rwanda. Kampala: Fountain Publishers.

Mkude, Daniel, Brian Cooksey and Lisbeth Levey (2003) Higher Education in Tanzania. Oxford: James Currey.

Moyo, Dambisa (2012) Winner Take All: China's Race for Resources and What it Means for Us. London: Allen Lane.

Moyo, Dambisa (2010) Dead Aid: Why Aid is not Working and How There is Another Way for Africa. London: Penguin Books.

Muzale, Henry (2006) Ikaningambo ya Oruhaya. Dar es Salaam: LOT Publications, p.175.

PBS. http://www.pbs.org/wgbh/pages/frontline/shows/rwanda/reports/refuse.html accessed 4th December, 2012.

Phillipson, Robert (1992) Linguistic Imperialism. Oxford: Oxford University Press.

Prunier, Gerard (1994) The Rwanda Crisis: History of a Genocide. Kampala: Fountain Publishers, p.172.

Rubagumya, Casmir (2010) Student Governance Systems and Practices in Tanzanian Universities. A Consultancy Report submitted to the Tanzania Commission for Universities.

Rubagumya, Casmir (2004) English in Africa and the emergence of Afro-Saxons: globalization or marginalization? In Baynham, M., A. Deignan and G. White (eds) Applied Linguistics at the Interface. London: Equinox/BAAL.

Rubagumya, Casmir (2000) Social and Political Dimensions of Choosing the Language of Instruction. Teaching Materials Developed for the World Bank Institute, Human Development Group, Washington D.C.

Rubagumya, Casmir, Okoth Okombo and Nazam Haloui (1997) Language of Instruction: Policy Implications for Education in Africa. Ottawa: IDRC.

Rubagumya, C.M. (ed.) (1994) Teaching and Researching Language in African Classrooms. Clevedon: Multilingual Matters.

Rubagumya, C.M. (1991) Language promotion for educational purposes: the example of Tanzania. International Review of Education 37(1) 67–87.

Rubagumya, C.M.(ed.) (1990) Language in Education in Africa. Clevedon: Multilingual Matters.

Rusagara, Frank (2009) Resilience of a Nation: A History of the Military in Rwanda. Kigali: Fountain Publishers.

Shivji, Issa G. (2012) Insha za Mapambano ya Wanyonge. Dar es Salaam: TUKI, pp. 222-223.

Printed in the United States
By Bookmasters